Wicca for Beginners

A Guide to Cultivating Real Wiccan Beliefs

(Useful for Improving Your and Your Loved Health and Happiness)

Merle Deckert

Published By **Chris David**

Merle Deckert

All Rights Reserved

Wicca for Beginners: A Guide to Cultivating Real Wiccan Beliefs (Useful for Improving Your and Your Loved Health and Happiness)

ISBN 978-1-77485-661-1

No part of this guidebook shall be reproduced in any form without permission in writing from the publisher except in the case of brief quotations embodied in critical articles or reviews.

Legal & Disclaimer

The information contained in this ebook is not designed to replace or take the place of any form of medicine or professional medical advice. The information in this ebook has been provided for educational & entertainment purposes only.

The information contained in this book has been compiled from sources deemed reliable, and it is accurate to the best of the Author's knowledge; however, the Author cannot guarantee its accuracy and validity and cannot be held liable for any errors or omissions. Changes are periodically made to this book. You must consult your doctor or get professional medical advice before using any of the suggested remedies, techniques, or information in this book.

Upon using the information contained in this book, you agree to hold harmless the Author from and against any damages, costs, and expenses, including any legal fees potentially resulting from the application of any of the information provided by this guide. This disclaimer applies to any damages or injury caused by the use and application, whether directly or indirectly, of any advice or information presented, whether for breach of contract, tort, negligence, personal injury, criminal intent, or under any other cause of action.

You agree to accept all risks of using the information presented inside this book. You need to consult a professional medical practitioner in order to ensure you are both able and healthy enough to participate in this program.

TABLE OF CONTENTS

Introduction 1

Chapter 1: What Exactly Is Wicca? 3

Chapter 2: The Basic Wiccan Faiths And Practices 15

Chapter 3: Traditional British Wicca/Lineaged Wicca 31

Chapter 4: Wiccan Traditions From All Over The World 41

Chapter 5: Practicing Wicca 63

Chapter 6: Getting Started Your Wiccan Practice 74

Chapter 7: History Of The Use Of Oils 85

Chapter 8: The Most Powerful Oils 119

Chapter 9: Using Stones And Crystals In Wicca 146

Chapter 10: Utilizing Oils In Witchcraft 151

Chapter 11: Utilizing Plants And Herbs In Witchcraft 153

Chapter 12: The Right Timing For Performing Rituals 157

Chapter 13: Designing Your Own Magickal Journal - Your Most Trusted Accountability Partner 160

Chapter 14: Tools For Wicca Practitioner 163

Chapter 15: Magical Circle And Sacred Altar 166

Chapter 16: Ritual To Destroy The Negativity That Is A Part Of Your Life ... 169

Chapter 17: The Journey Of The Witch: Walking A Path Of Wicca 173

Chapter 18: Wiccan Candle Magick 176

Conclusion 183

Introduction

If you've ever been interested about Wicca or thought about studying Wicca or perhaps you just want to learn more about the details of what Wicca is about, then this is the right book for you. From a background of Wicca to how to begin creating your very own Wiccan practices, "Wicca for Beginners" provides all the essential details on this intriguing and important system of belief. The other topics covered include the differences between the traditional and multifaceted Wiccan rituals, as well as a brief description of some of the key Wiccan practices, and an introduction to some of the main Wiccan practices.

If you're unfamiliar with this belief system, Wicca can seem obscure and distinct from other, more popular religions. Wicca is often confused with other religions like Satanism and Luciferianism. This leads to misperceptions regarding the unique Wiccan principles and beliefs. But, like many other religions, Wicca has its own deep history, culture and set of beliefs. Although Wicca isn't as popular in the same way as Judaism, Christianity, or Islam however, it is an extremely meaningful spiritual or religious system that is used by hundreds of hundreds of thousands. It is a religion that combines rituals, magic and belief in gods self-awareness, as well as spiritual development.

Thank you for buying this book. And please take your time reading!

Chapter 1: What Exactly Is Wicca?

The first practice that was officially recognized as Wicca is generally thought to have started during the 30s of the United Kingdom, but the religious practice has its theological roots in the 19th century, and more importantly in the witch hunts of the later Middle Ages.

Witches who were vilified in the latter part of the Middle Ages in Europe were typically regarded as Satanists worshippers of the devil who had renounced the main Christian religion of the period. The early 19th century however, some researchers argued that these people were not been adherents of Satan and were rather followers of a pagan religion pre-Christian that endured through the Middle Ages. These theories advanced and eventually became the focus of numerous books, among them Aradia or The Gospel of the Witches, written by Charles Leland in 1899, as well as The Witch-Cult in Western Europe (1921) and The God of the Witches (1933) both written composed by Margaret Murray. This was the theory that became the foundation of the basis from which Wicca was born and early followers claimed that they were the relics of the pre-Christian pagan religion.

The pagan-based religion that later became Wicca began to emerge during the 40s and 50s of England. Gerald Gardner, an amateur Anthropologist who was also a former British civil employee with a particular passion for the occult and pagan religions established the Bricket Wood coven. Gardner claimed that he was admitted into the pagan coven known as the New Forest coven, in Hampshire, England, in the latter part of 1930. Following his move from Bricket Wood, he decided to form a coven nearer the home he was living in. He found a naturalist-oriented club known as The Fiveacres Country Club, and some of the members were his first initiators. It was the Bricket Wood coven would prove to be extremely influential as Wicca became more popular because some participants would later influence the growth and expansion of Wicca's religion. In the early days the term

"Wicca" did not commonly used to describe the beliefs which was practiced by coven members. Gardner prefers the words "witch cult" "witchcraft," and the "Old Religion." Gardner didhowever, at times, use the term to refer to those who practiced their religion under the name of "the Wica."

Gardner died in 1964, however his legacy remained in the hands of many important members belonging to The Bricket Wood coven. Doreen Valiente Dafo, Frederick Lamond, Jack Bracelin, Dayonis, Lois Bourne, and Eleanor Bone would all go to establish different covens and carry on the practice of Gardner's convictions. In the late 1950s the religion was beginning to be referred to in the form of "Wicca," a word that is derived of"witch," an Old English word for "sorcerer" or "witch." It had already seen its first major division. Gardner's initial attempts to create The Bricket Wood coven were secretly kept, but in the 1950s, he started to look for publicity. The coven's other members disagreed to this and, in the year 1957 some members, like Gardner's high priestess Doreen Valiente were able to decide to separate and establish the coven of their own. While there were differences of opinion on some matters however, coven members of the Bricket Wood coven , as well as newly formed coven were based on the traditional, "Gardnerian," principles.

In England, Wicca spread to the remainder of the British Isles and from there to other regions of the globe, including Australia as well as Australia and the United States. The new followers of Gardner's religion frequently merged his ideas with regional pagan beliefs which led to the creation of new types of Wicca. Alexandrian Wicca, Dianic Wicca as well as The Feri Tradition, the 1734 Tradition and many others developed from these new versions of Gardnerian Wicca (see Chapter 4 for more information). The forms of Wicca that adhere to Gardner's initial vision are often described as "British traditional Wicca," while other types of Wicca are usually referred to as "eclectic."

In the last decade of the 20th century Wicca gained more recognition and was able to influence the popular culture. Books such as Mastering Witchcraft, published in 1970 by Paul Hudson, taught those interested in Wicca how to become member of this religion and without regard to any coven. This was the catalyst to the rise of an multi-faceted Wicca. The subsequent books about Wicca were typically inspired by the writings and beliefs of the early Wicca practitioners, including the first high priestess of Gardner, Doreen Valiente. They also promoted self-initiation. The concept of Wicca or the practice of witchcraft as a general religion was made popular by films such as The Craft, which came out in 1996, as well as popular television shows such as Charmed that was on from 1998 until 2006.

The internet became increasingly well-known and accessible in the decade of 2000, Wiccan groups began to move online. Wiccan leaders like Silver RavenWolf aimed their efforts at those who were young and who were interested in religion and witchcraft practices. Wicca was subsequently associated with that New Age movement that gained recognition during the same period and Wiccan beliefs became to be "trendy." There was a protest against this brand popular, new Wicca emerged within the Wiccan community, which led to revivalist Wicca movement that was founded in Gardnerian and other earlier Wiccan faith systems.

There are up to 800,000 practicing Wiccans all over the world. Many adhere to very conventional, Gardnerian forms of Wicca While others are influenced by newer or more eclectic practices. There are covens that belong to certain groups and others choose to adhere to Wicca independently. Wicca is a distinct among other religions due to the fact that it promotes doubt, even about its personal beliefs, practices and beliefs and is usually open to individual practice. There are probably to be as many different kinds associated with Wicca in the same way as people who practice the Craft. Each of them are rooted in pre-Christian European pagan religions and all share some degree of influences of Gardner.

What isn't Wicca?

The meaning of "Wicca" can be a subject of contention in the minds of numerous Wiccans as well as non-wiccans. Some believe that the term"Wicca" only applies for British Traditional Wicca and that any other "eclectic" Wiccan tradition should not be referred to as Wiccan even if it is a Wiccan tradition. Certain diverse traditions make use of the term, while other traditions do not. Many people disavow their affiliation with Wicca and see it as being purely Gardnerian Some feel that the significance of the word is diluted through fads and insincerity and the popularity associated with New Age religions in general. In these instances the word "Wicca" is generally used as well as in a academic sense. It's helpful to those studying neopaganism for them to classify neopagan belief systems that have their source in United Kingdom under one umbrella name, "Wicca." As as a result, some of the groups listed in Chapter 4 wouldn't identify themselves as Wiccan.

Beyond the argument over what groups should or should not be classified as Wiccan There are a few neopagan beliefs that differ from Wicca. There are other beliefs that are not compatible with Wicca. Wicca differs than Satanism and Luciferianism but certain groups that fall under the Wiccan umbrella acknowledge a god or gods that are similar to these religions. Wicca is not like Thelema which was a religion established through Aleister Crowley during the first decade of 1900. Gardner was influenced by his writings, many of which he employed in the early Wiccan rituals. The difference is that Thelema is one of the religions that values the freedom of will over all else, acknowledges an ancient pantheon that is based on Egyptian gods, and uses the art of magick (Crowley's prefered spelling) to develop freedom of will. Wicca has more variety than Thelema , and the concept of freedom of will is the main focus the importance of self-awareness, responsibility as well as spiritual growth are more significant. Thelema is not part of Wicca since it was established prior to when Wicca was founded. Other theories that have influenced other Wiccan practices include Qabalah as well as The Hermetic Order of the Golden Dawn, Freemasonry, Druidry as well as classical mythology along with folk and traditional magic. If taken as a whole all of these religions or philosophies are part of Wicca however they share a lot with certain Wiccan practices. There are other witchcraft traditions that aren't Wiccan usually because they came from various times and at various places. They comprise Stregheria (Italian witchcraft), Jewitchery (Jewish mysticism and witchcraft), Polytheistic Reconstructionism (a recreation of the ancient witchcraft), Kitchen Witchcraft, Hedge Witchcraft, and Asatru (Norse witchcraft).

Certain aspects are fundamental to the practice of religion, which is known as "Wiccan." The first of them is that of the use of magic. The majority of Wiccan traditions make use of magic in a certain way. Someone that believed in similar gods as part of a Wiccan tradition, followed the same rituals and believed in the same philosophy, but that did not believe in the magic's power to create changes in the world would never be considered Wiccan. A faith in the supernatural at a certain way is generally required for being Wiccan. Although Wicca is extremely accepting of different interpretations of God as well as the archetypal interpretation which allows people to view divinities as expressions of our unconscious the absence of faith in a supernatural power that is beyond human awareness or comprehension could render Wiccan practices difficult. For certain Wiccans who do not subscribe to Wiccan Rede or the Law of Threefold Return is a reason to disqualify other people of being Wiccan. But not all Wiccans believe that these concepts are vital to their belief in the religion.

Although Wicca is very compatible with other belief systems, and particularly those which have at some point or another had an influence on the various traditions of Wicca in its own right but it is not compatible with many of the major religions in the world. Religions such as Judaism, Christianity, and Islam which believe in one powerful, all-powerful God and deny the worship of other gods, typically are inclined to consider Wicca as well as other religions similar to it as atheistic. They also do not approve of the use of magic, believing it as the work of Satan. Since the Judeo-Christian as well as Muslim God has all power, He should be the ultimate source of all worldly changes and aid. Magic takes the power of the hands of God and is therefore considered to be sinful. The incompatibility doesn't, however, mean that it is not possible to be a part of certain Christian Wiccans, for example. There is, in actual an ancient form of Wicca that is known as Trinitarian Wicca that follows the Wiccan calendar and presides over the Christian pantheon which includes a goddess (see chapter 4). There is evidence that suggests a mixture between Jewish as well as Wiccan beliefs, as in Muslim or Wiccan beliefs are possible, but in all three instances, the practitioners have to deal with contradictions, incongruities and challenging questions.

Chapter 2: The Basic Wiccan Faiths And Practices

Theology of Duotheism

The majority, but not all Wiccans are worshippers of two gods The Mother Goddess and the Horned God. Both of these figures are believed to be the gods that were worshipped by hunters and gatherers in Europe in the Stone Age, whose veneration was passed over the centuries until the present day. Both the Mother Goddess as well as the God of Horns are believed to be embodied forces manifesting themselves in nature, similar to that of the Taoist beliefs in the yin as well as Yang.

It is believed that the Wiccan Horned God usually connected to the natural world and particularly the animal kingdom. The Wiccan Horned God is thought to be the perfect man's role model. In certain Wiccan tradition, he's often referred to as the Oak King The Sun God, the Love God and The Lord of Death or the Leader in the Wild Hunt instead of the Horned God. She is usually associated with spring, fertility and life. Certain Wiccans consider their Goddess as a three-deity comprised of the Maiden Goddess (symbolizing virginity) as well as the mother Goddess (symbolizing the fertility) as well as Crone Goddess (symbolizing wisdom). Some portray her as a Menstrual Goddess or Moon Goddess. Gardner believed that the Horned God as well as the Mother Goddess to be the vehicles for cosmic power, in that they assisted humans come in contact with the power of that energy.

Wiccan beliefs are varied, which means that not all Wiccans are strictly duotheists. In reality, Wiccans can be pantheist or polytheist, monotheist as well as atheist. Gardner himself was a bit of a pantheistic view of Wiccan gods and believed that a god too complicated to comprehend by humans existed and developed"the" Horned God and the Mother Goddess. Gardner did not, however believe that this entity often referred to as the "Supreme Deity,"" "Prime Mover,"" "Cosmic Logos," or "Godhead," was otherwise active in the lives of human beings. Some Wiccans think that both the Horned God and the Mother Goddess are two facets of a pantheistic world in which every aspect of existence is a manifestation from the Divine. There are theistic Wiccans believe that each goddess is a part that of Mother Goddess as well as that each god is a part that of God Horned. Some theistic Wiccans believe that many gods and goddesses exist, however that they are distinct in their own distinct entity. While Gardner along with his followers was against monotheistic Wiccans and their monotheistic beliefs, they were not against the monotheistic Wiccans. Church of Wicca in the United States worships one genderless god, while those who follow the Dianic Wiccan tradition Wicca is a worship of one god. Additionally, some Wiccans consider that the many gods and goddesses associated with Wicca are not real instead, they are archetypes or ideas generated in the collective consciousness that are resonated through rituals. These Wiccans can technically be classified as atheists.

This diversity of beliefs can be difficult to categorize Wicca as a pure duotheistic religion. But since most Wiccans acknowledge the existence, either literal or archetypal God and Goddess regardless of whether their view of God is more polytheistic or pantheistic this religion can be likely to be viewed as duotheistic.

Magic

Wiccans believe that magic (sometimes called "magick") to refer to a form of force that can be utilized to influence various situations by means of witchcraft. The precise mechanisms through which magic operates are a subject of debate within Wiccans who believe that it's the manipulation of hidden natural forces and the ability to channel willpower to create changes, or just the application of the normal five senses. Others Wiccans aren't concerned about how magic works, believing in its power based upon the evidence that they have seen.

Wiccans have always been concerned about the concept of magic within their faith. The early Wiccans described the type of magic they used in the form of "white magic" to distinguish it from "black magic" used by Satanists or any other group that is thought to be associated with evil. Other Wiccans made the same distinction, referring to magic that had positive intent being"the "right-hand route" and spells with negative intentions being"left hand path. "left-hand route." A few contemporary Wiccans oppose this term and argue that left-handedness or the color black is a prerequisite for negative or evil intentions.

Wiccan rituals are different in their rituals, but they all follow the same setting, with an altarthat is often ornamented by images depicting the Horned God or Mother Goddess as well as a set of magic tools. Essential tools of magic include the wand, a chalice and a pentacle (a symbol of talismanism that is engraved with the pentagram) and a shorter knife, known as an athameand a cauldron candles, incense, and a besom, also known as a the broomstick. Some of the tools are required to complete a magic ritual. Wiccans can also choose their tools according to the intention of the ritual.

While Wiccan rituals, just like the other elements of Wicca are different, British Traditional Wicca does follow a traditional ritual. The ritual begins by cleansing the space that will be used for the ritual as well as the participants during the ceremony. It can be a straightforward method to cleanse the space and remove negative energy as well as ritual bathing or even a period of fasting. After that, the participants create a circle. A circle is a space of protection which helps Wiccans connect with divinity. Circle casting was designed as part of a magical ritual through members of the Bricket Wood Coven who discovered it to be extremely effective, however, it's not a requirement for the purpose of magic. Thirdly, practitioners make calls in the realm of the elements. The majority of Wiccans adhere to the five classic elements: earth, water air, fire, and aether, also known as spirit. The four first classic elements are linked to cardsinal direction: north and earth water with west and south, while fire is associated with south while air is associated with the east. Aether is the center element that is the one element that unites all the other elements. The chanting of the elements during an occult ritual is typically represented by placing a symbol of each element's center of the circle. Then, the participants form an edifice of power. Cone of Power is a method through which Wiccans increase their energy levels for the purpose of a ritual. To increase the power cone, participants form an arc, clasp hands, and concentrate on the point that is that is above that of their circle. Dance, music or other ritual actions can be performed to increase the energy levels and the cones of strength. When the energy is raised by the power cone the Wiccans can invoke to the Horned God or Mother Goddess and their powers, which they can use to enhance their own magic. When the gods are present and the energy have been rekindled the participants are able to use the spell and "workings." Wiccans commonly use spells to ensure protection or fertility, healing or positive energy, however spells can come in any shape. Spellcasting is usually accompanied in certain Wiccan practices through an act known as the Great Rite: ritualized sexual interaction between the High Priest and the High Priestess, who summoned Horned God and Goddess to enslave them. The majority of times this Great Rite is performed symbolically by using an athame as well as the crystal chalice. The athame represents God the Horned God while the chalice is a symbol of that of the mother Goddess. It is the Great Rite, like the raising of the cone of power is intended to boost energy to spellcast. It is believed that spellcasting as well as the Great Rite are sometimes followed by dancing, chanting, games or wine, as well as food. The ritual is concluded with a goodbye to the gods and the four elements. Finally, the circle is ceremonially closed.

There are many variations of Wiccan rituals are based on the elaborate patterns laid in British Traditional Wicca. Rituals may be brief and require more concentration than symbolic rites, dancing and singing. It is not necessary to gather a large number of participants to carry out the ritual. Spellcasting and circle casting can be carried out by single practitioners or in groups. The details of rituals differ from tradition to tradition , and the coven and coven. The Gardner's Bricket Wood coven, and later Gardnerian Wiccan traditions, are well-known for performing rituals with magic in the naked which is also known as "skyclad." It is believed that this custom could be a result of reality it was Bricket Wood was a naturalist club before Gardner bought it and began covens there. Some Wiccans wear robes, or even street clothing.

Wheel of the Year Wheel of the Year

Wiccan rituals can be observed at any timeof the year, but Wiccans are also able to observe a variety of religious holidays, or Sabbats, which they observe all through the year. The entire collection of these festivals is referred to as"the "Wheel of the year." The majority of Wiccans observe eight Sabbats however, some only observe the four or six. The first Wiccans were only celebrating four Sabbats that are known as "Greater Sabbats." These are also known as the "cross-quarter days" which are the midpoints between the solstice, equinox and the equinox. They are the Greater Sabbats are Samhain, observed on October 31st and November 1st Imbolc and February 1st, or 2nd, Beltane that is which is celebrated from April 30th until May 1st and Lughnasadh which is which is celebrated on July 31st or the 1st of August. Samhain is connected to deaths and with the ancestral spirits. Imbolc is the time to see beginning signs of spring. Beltane which is the time of full spring bloom as well as Lughnasadh which is the time of first fruit.

Wiccans who observe only four Sabbats, celebrate those 4 Greater Sabbats. Wiccans who observe longer than 4 Sabbats celebrate solstices and solstices, which are known as "Lesser Sabbats." The celebration of solstices and equinoxes was first introduced in 1958. those who were part of the Bricket Wood coven decided that they would observe these holidays along with those of the Greater Sabbats. These Lesser Sabbats are Yuletide, observed on the 21st of December, or 22nd Ostara which is observed on March 21st or 22, Litha which is celebrated June 21st or 22nd and Mabon which is observed on September 21st or 22nd.

For those living in the Southern Hemisphere, the Wiccan Wheel of the Year is reversed so that the celebrations coincide with the correct season. So, for instance, Samhain is celebrated from April 30th through May 1st. Yuletide is celebrated on the 21st of June.

Wiccan traditional ceremonies that are held for the Greater Sabbats and Lesser Sabbats, but particularly the Greater Sabbats are usually believed to be a reference to pagan pagan ceremonies that existed prior to the Christian era. This could or might not be the case, and because Wicca is spreading, a lot people believe that Sabbat celebrations have adopted different, more universal features that are dependent on the specific culture within which Wicca is rooted. The Wiccan names for Sabbats are often based on Gaelic Polytheism, as well as Germanic pagan beliefs, however the ceremonies themselves could differ partly because there isn't much historical evidence concerning religious festivals from the early days of Christianity. Europe.

Apart from the seven Greater Sabbats, and the eight Lesser Sabbats, Wiccans celebrate Esbats. Esbats are any celebration that is not a Sabbat. Esbat could refer to any other celebration that is not any Sabbats However, Esbat is usually used to refer to the Wiccan celebrations during the full moon. Although Sabbats and Esbats both Sabbats and Esbats are a part of rituals, Sabbats are more times of celebration, whereas Esbats are more mystical work and spell casting as in addition to any administrative tasks that covens have to perform. If a coven performs ceremonies for initiation, they're typically performed during Esbats. Wiccans celebrate Esbats since they believe that the moon's fullness is the most powerful time to perform magic. However, the new moon is when magic is the weakest. Certain Wiccans don't perform magic in any way during this time however, others may use the Esbat that has a distinct emphasis. Apart from being the Wheel of the Year, the 13 yearly cycles of mood are the most significant element of the Wiccan calendar.

The Wiccan Rede

In contrast to many other religions, which include the most popular religions in the world, Wicca has few rules and regulations regarding morality. The most well-known principle for Wiccan morality is called"the" Wiccan Rede, which says: "An' it harm nobody, do as you want." This Wiccan Rede is generally interpreted as an acceptance of free will and is accompanied by a warning that any action has consequences. Wiccans should think about the consequences prior to acting, and accept the responsibility for their actions after they have taken them. The notion that freewill is very important to Wiccans as anyone who forces on the wishes of another person is believed to be causing harm and thus infringing on Wiccan Rede. Wiccan Rede. Because of this, Wiccans consider that magic, regardless of good or evil nature, shouldn't be applied to another in the absence of consent from the person to the ceremony. Any magic that is performed on another without their consent could be incompatible with their individual will and may cause harm.

The origins for Wiccan Rede's origins Wiccan Rede is unknown, however, similar formulas for morality and free will may be found in other works of literature. French Renaissance writer physician, scholar and doctor Francois Rabelais wrote, "fay what you wantdras," archaic French for "do whatever you want." Gardner compared the Wiccan Rede to the ethic of King Pausol "Do whatever you want so that you do not harm anyone." It is also a reference to the philosophy of King Pausol. Wiccan Rede also has similarities to the religious philosophy of Thelema, where free will plays a significant part.

In addition to The Wiccan Rede, some Wiccans adhere to The Law of Threefold Return, which is like the Eastern concept of the concept of karma. According to the Law of Threefold Return states that every action taken by an individual will be returned for them multiple times. The good and the bad deeds are magnified three times. Certain Wiccans are also trying to cultivate eight virtues which are cited in the work of Doreen Valiente, in the liturgical text "Charge of the Goddess." The eight virtues include compassion, beauty, power, strength as well as humility, honor respect, and joy. In addition, certain Wiccans particularly those who adhere to British Traditional Wicca, follow the 161 laws known as the Ardanes. Some Wiccans disapprove of the rules as antiquated and unproductive They also claim that they were created through Gardner early in his career to give him more the power of his original coven.

The early Wiccans were divided over the subject of homosexuality, however Wiccans nowadays are generally accepting and encourage all gender expressions and sexuality. They often base their opinions in The Wiccan Rede.

Chapter 3: Traditional British Wicca/Lineaged Wicca

Like the other faiths Wicca includes a variety of denominations that have different traditions, histories and practices. These denominations are known as "traditions." The traditions differ in significant ways, from those who adhere to very strict rules and regulations as well as those that are more relaxed in their practices. The most rigorous of Wiccan practices are referred to by the name of "British Traditional Wicca" or, more often "Lineaged Wicca." In British Traditional Wiccan traditions, everyone is initiated and are able to trace their lineage through Gerald Gardner. This chapter will explain in greater detail the Wiccan traditions considered as part of British Traditional Wicca.

Gardnerian Wicca

Gardnerian Wicca has its roots and its roots go back directly into Gerald Gardner and the New Forest coven, where Gardner was initiated into the early 1930s. Gardnerian covens adhere to the rules and edicts established in the 1930s by Gardner himself. Gardnerian covens are usually limited to thirteen members however, this is more of a suggestion rather than a standard. Each coven is led by the High Priestess as well as an High Priest who are able to trace their initial family tree through Gardner himself. They are the ones responsible for introducing new members into the coven. Gardner developed his rites and rituals that he devised in the name of Wicca on the rituals that were practiced by his New Forest coven where he was initiated in addition to the writings and practices of folklorists and occultists. His goal was to keep this practice in Britain in the way he discovered it, a method which he believed to have been handed down since pre-Christian times. Since Gardner became the very first person to create Wicca in the form of a faith instead of an ad-hoc ritual and was considered to be the founder of Wicca and the entire Wiccan practices, regardless of traditional British Wicca or the more diverse Wicca as well as solitary practices are a part of their history to him as well as Gardnerian Wicca in general.

Members from Gardnerian Wicca pass through three stages of initative. The initial degree of initiation is welcoming members to join a coven . It also involves an intensive research into the rituals and history of the religion. Participants who progress into the next degree may be initiated as the first degree of members from their. Third Degree Wiccans are referred to as High Priests or High Priestesses. They are able to create their own, separate covens. Third-degree Wiccan can start both second and first-degree Wiccans however second degree Wiccans are only able to initiate those who are of those of the initial degree. Gardnerians typically adhere to cross-gendered initiations, where priests are initiated by priestesses and vice versa.

Gardnerian Wicca is a tradition that is referred to by the name of "oathbound;" in other terms, many of the rituals and practices aren't available to people who haven't received initiation into the Craft.

This practice is associated with the notion of Mystery. The Mystery is an idea that is not explained. It must be felt, and every person is able to experience and comprehend this Mystery through their unique unique way. Rituals used in Gardnerian Wicca are the means that practitioners can feel and appreciate the Mystery.

Gardnerian Wicca is also "orthopraxic," as opposed to "orthodoxic." Orthopraxic religion is not dogmatic, and is based on proper practice as opposed to an orthodoxy-based religion that focuses on correct thinking. This means that Gardnerian Wiccans can be duotheists or monotheists, pantheists or polytheists, as well as have other belief systems regarding gods. It is their commitment to the right application of Gardnerian Wiccan rituals and rites that make them a integral part of tradition instead of a particular collection of beliefs. Many religions have proper belief systems lead to proper practices. For instance, in Gardnerian Wicca, correct practice is a result of belief.

However within the limits of Wiccan Rede, no belief is considered "right" as opposed to "wrong." It is a general rule but Gardnerian Wiccans recognize two Gods: the Mother Goddess and the Horned God.

Gardnerian Wicca uses a Book of Shadows that includes many of the rituals and rituals. Newcomers to the religion are usually asked to create (sometimes using a pen) their individual versions from the Book of Shadows. Different variations of the Book of Shadows exist for various Wiccan styles and practices, however Gardnerians make use of this version. It is the Book of Shadows that was developed by Gardner along the High Priestess Doreen Valiente. Gardner declared that the usage of this book was common among witches of all times and was handed down through time. The evidence to support the claim isn't clear however, and Gardner could have in fact invented the concept himself. The first book he wrote was titled "Ye Bok of Ye Art Magical" as well as The Book of Shadows that eventually became canon was extensively edited and modified by Valiente. It is believed that the Book of Shadows plays an important function in the lives of Gardnerian Wiccans and is considered an oathbound book, and is not given to non-Wiccans. However, the majority of it was released with the consent of Valiente in the late 1980s.

In the end, Gardnerian Wicca has a long-standing tradition of keeping secrets. Certain lineages that belong to Gardnerian Wiccans are publicly known and Gardner himself was keen on publicizing his work to preserve the status quo of the Craft however, Gardnerian Wiccans often keep their coven membership secret. Members are not allowed to disclose details of their personal information or the membership status of other members of a coven without the person's explicit permission. In some instances this may be for security reasons. Wiccans often refer to themselves as being either in or out within their "broom closet" to refer to their openness to their beliefs.

Alexandrian Wicca

Alexandrian Wicca is another tradition that is believed as part of British Traditional Wicca. It was created around the year 1960 in United Kingdom by Alex and Maxine Sanders. Their name for the religion comes from both the name of the founder and from the mythical Library of Alexandria. Alexandrian Wicca shares many similarities in common with Gardnerian Wicca because Alex Sanders was an early Gardnerian initiate prior to starting his own custom. Yet, Alexandrian Wicca also includes aspects of ritual magic that aren't found with Gardnerian Wicca and is influenced by the Hermetic Qabalah.

Similar to Gardnerian Wicca, Alexandrian Wicca is an initiation process that allows people to become members of the tradition. it has three stages of init members can reach. In certain Alexandrian covens, there's the fourth level, referred to in"the "neophyte" which is also known as "dedicant" grade. Neophytes and dedicants don't swear oaths, but are permitted to participate in aspects of ritual and ritual that aren't bound by oaths. This way they can be a part of the Alexandrian tradition prior to taking a vow of commitment. If they choose to be initiated into in the initial degree of membership, they'll become a part within the traditions.

The main distinction in Alexandrian or Gardnerian Wicca is that the earlier places more focus on ceremonial magic. Ceremonial magic is broad and encompasses the magic rituals used in all types of Wicca which are both the traditional and the diverse. In Alexandrian Wicca ritual magic is a greater part than in other Wiccan practices. Magic is also performed more loosely than Gardnerian Wicca and Sanders telling his followers "if the magic works try this method." Alexandrian Wiccan magic rituals are often by skyclad, however this isn't as prevalent as in Gardnerian Wicca and generally employ instruments similar to the ones employed for Gardnerian rituals. As with Gardner, Sanders wrote a personal Book of Shadows that has been copied and passed on across the world of Wiccan. Because Sanders altered the Book of Shadows multiple times during his life, several variations of Alexandrian versions are available.

Alexandrian ritual magic also incorporates elements from The Hermetic Qabalah, a Western mystic tradition of the occult which began to emerge during the Middle Ages. It is believed that the Qabalah can be found in various varieties, been a part of Judaism, Christianity, Platonism and Gnosticism. In recent times it has been incorporated in the philosophical theories associated with New Age movements, Neopaganism and, of course Wicca. The main tenets of the Qabalah are the divine energy flow and divinity's nature, and the methods of discerning the divine. The basic concept behind these beliefs is similar to the notions of "raising the energy" and bringing in the presence of gods that are central to Wiccan rituals.

Alexandrian Wicca has spread across to the United Kingdom, and covens are found throughout Australia, Canada and the United States, Canada, and Australia.

Algard Tradition

The Algard Tradition of Wicca was established around 1972, in 1972 by Mary Nesnick. Nesnick was an American High Priestess as well as was an initiator in the two traditions of Gardnerian as well as Alexandrian Wicca. Her Algard Tradition was her attempt to join these two which are already very similar in their practices. This is why it shares traits with both. In this way, it is similar to both. Algard Tradition is considered part of British Traditional Wicca because its practitioners can trace their earliest roots all the way back to Gardner.

Chapter 4: Wiccan Traditions From All Over The World

Contrary the tradition of British Traditional Wicca, in which practitioners trace their roots to Gardner the diverse Wicca practices have a variety of roots. They were often founded by witches who were studying or involved in lineage tradition. Others were created by those who were practicing hereditary magic or learned about Wicca through other methods. Certain Wiccans have their own rituals for initiation and others permit self-initiation, or don't need initiation in any way. Eclectic Wiccans may also be "solitaries," or witches who are solely practicing. Solitaries aren't often British Traditional Wiccans, simply because a coven is required for both lineage and the ability to initiate. This chapter will provide a brief overview of different Wiccan traditions and will highlight various ways that the diverse Wicca may differ with British Traditional Wicca.

Seax-Wica

Seax-Wica is a form of Wicca which was established in 1973 by Raymond Buckland in 1973. Buckland was an ex- Gardnerian high priest of British origin who immigrated from the UK to United States and decided to create the eponymous Wiccan tradition that was based on Anglo-Saxon pagan beliefs. Seax-Wicca isn't a reconstructed version of the religion practised by the Anglo-Saxons. It utilizes their iconography and certain of the principles that are a part of Gardnerian Wicca.

Seax-Wica has four gods named Woden, Thunor, Freya and Tiw. Woden (often known as Odin) is the principal god of Norse as well as Germanic mythology that is often linked to healing, knowledge poetry, sorcery, and death. Thunor (also Thor) is a Norse and Germanic god of strong, storms protection, fertility, and storms. Freya is an Norse goddess who is associated with love, beauty, fertility, and sexual sex as well as fertility. Tiw is the Germanic god of the law and glory. All four deities are believed to be representations of the two principal Wiccan gods that are the Horned God and the Mother Goddess.

Initiation and hierarchy are less significant in Seax-Wica as it is in Gardnerian Wicca, Alexandrian Wicca as well as in the Algard Tradition. Seax-Wica new practitioners are able to get initiated through covens however, it is also permissible for individuals to dedicate themselves to the tradition. Likewise, the process of initiation isn't required for anyone to be a member of Seax-Wica. The non-censored publication of Buckland's Seax-Wica book helps to open up the tradition. Seax-Wica covens favour democracy over the system of hierarchy when choosing their the leaders. Coven officers, which include the "thegn," or sergeant-at-arms who oversees the building of the coven, as well as the scribe who maintains the records of the coven, are elected by coven's members. Both the High Priest and High Priestess from each coven are elected as well. The elected leaders are removed from office and substituted.

While Buckland who was the Seax-Wica founder, has been initiated in Gardnerian Wicca, the Seax-Wica tradition is not considered to be part of British Traditional Wicca because of the possibility of self-initiation. To be considered part the tradition of British Traditional Wicca, traditions have to have to be "lineaged," that is that each participant is required to trace their origins all the way back to Gardner himself. Seax-Wica has a lot in common with the practices that are part of British Traditional Wicca, but it's not a lineage-based tradition.

Dianic Wicca

Dianic Wicca is a feminist tradition of Wicca created by Zsuzsanna Budapest, and named in honor of Diana, the Roman goddess Diana. Budapest was first initiated to the world of magic and witchcraft through her mom in their home country of Hungary was heavily engaged in feminist movements in the 1970s. She also developed the official religion of Dianic Wicca, in part, in response to laws against witchcraft in the State of California. Her aim was to place the Craft on the same level as other religions that were more popular. Prior to that, she was the creator of Susan B. Anthony Coven #1, a coven for women which was only open to women.

Dianic Wicca takes many elements from British Traditional Wicca. Dianic Wiccans follow the Wiccan Wheel of the Year, celebration of all 4 Greater Sabbats and the four Lesser Sabbats. They perform various rites and employ various ritual tools. Yet, Dianic Wicca varies significantly from other traditions in the sense that practitioners worship only one god or goddess, and covens are comprised exclusively of women.

Since they believe in only one female god the people who practice Dianic Wicca can be considered monotheists in their beliefs, however they worship goddesses of many religions and cultures and believe that they all be facets of one goddess. Dianic Wiccans may also view the Goddess as a trinity comprised of the Maiden Goddess, a Mother Goddess and a Crone Goddess. The Goddess is believed to be the source of all living creatures and as the goddess of protection for women. Dianic Wiccans appeal to the Goddess by using magical techniques such as meditation, visualization and other more traditional spellwork. Many times rituals are used to empower women, reduce the patriarchal standards of society and help heal personal trauma. While certain Dianic Wiccans believe that it is acceptable to tie or even extort women, for example, sexual predators through spell casting, other Wiccans believe the practice to be in contradiction with traditional Wiccan Rede and the exercise of the freedom of choice.

Due to its female-dominated grouping and its emphasis on sexuality of females, Dianic Wicca is often attracted by bisexual and lesbian women, but the tradition accepts heterosexual women too. Budapest has herself been a lesbian as are a few of rituals are designed to encourage women to explore their sexuality within a space that is not of the control of men. Certain covens challenge gender roles as a general rule as well as promoting an unwavering connection between body and gender but exclude transgender people. While the majority of Dianic Wiccans belong to covens however, there are some who are sole practitioners who were in the spirit of Budapest's writings and philosophical ideas.

"Dianic Wicca" is a term that refers to the practice of "Dianic Wicca" is sometimes also used to refer to a particular tradition that was founded by Morgan McFarland and Mark Roberts. The tradition restricts leadership in covens to women, however the High Priestess of each coven can decide whether or not to accept males as practitioners. Like Budapest's Dianic Wicca, McFarland's Dianic Wicca is founded on feminist principles.

Feri Tradition

The Feri Tradition of Wicca was created through Victory Henry and Cora Anderson the American couple around the year 1960. It's not element of British Traditional Wicca but is generally considered to be an official Wiccan tradition due to its ties to contemporary pagan witchcraft. It is believed that both Victor Henry and Cora were adept at witchcraft and magic prior to meeting in the first place, with Cora having been raised in a household that used folk magic. Both claimed to have initially met in the realm of the astral. The 1950s were when they read Gardner's writings Gerald Gardner and became interested in forming their coven of their own. Gwydion Pendderwen is a close family friend who was later accepted into the Andersons coven, and brought certain features that were part of Alexandrian Wicca into the nascent tradition. Feri has also included elements of Huna which is an ancient New Age religion based on the ethnic Hawaiian beliefs, Voodoo, and the background of the individual followers. Its name for the Andersons tradition was at first not, Feri, but rather Vicia. But, Victor Henry spoke so often about Celtic magical and natural spirits, that the term "fairy" was associated with the practices of the Andersons. It was the spelling "Feri" was used in the late 1990s to distinguish the practice from other forms of witchcraft, which could have the same name.

Feris do not adhere to The Wiccan Rede and do not believe in the Law of Threefold Return. They consider that the individual is responsible for the results for their decisions. They don't have the standard Book of Shadows; rather they share their beliefs by oral tradition and practitioners are able to create themselves spellbooks, or even add to those written by other people. Rituals and rules of initiation are not as strict than those of British Traditional Wicca. The process of initiating can differ from coven to coven, however, initiation itself typically is a one-step procedure.

One of the major distinctions between Feri and more conventional Wiccan practices is the fact that Feris put more focus on worshipping diverse, sexually diverse gods while the practices of British Traditional Wicca focus on the dual nature of female and male gods. This is in part due to this difference, Feri has been called as an "ecstatic" tradition, whereas other Wiccan practices are "fertility" practices. The main Feri god has been identified as being The Star Goddess, who is the source of all that is that exists in the universe. It is believed that she is the basis of each other god and that the gods are in turn aspects of her being. Certain Feris think that she's not female, but more pansexual. The concept of a singular god from whom all gods are born can be compared with what is known as the Gardnerian belief in the existence of a "Supreme deity." Alongside Feris' belief in the Star Goddess, Feris worship the lemniscate gods, which are six gods that are considered to be the reflections or children from The Star Goddess. Feris have also placed a large amount of importance in the concept about the Divine Twins, who are simultaneously the children and lovers to God of the Star Goddess. The gods of the six lemniscate can be twinned to symbolize those of the Divine Twins or be represented as twins themselves. The Feri gods and their relations to one another and with themselves can be a bit contradictory which is a characteristic Feri believers embrace as being meaningful. Feris can also identify with other gods or have different names for gods they believe in. The belief system is pantheistic since all gods are believed as being aspects that are part of Star Goddess, and polytheistic as many gods are revered.

Since Feri can be described as an exalted religion Rituals are typically created to bring the participants directly into contact with gods through sensual experiences and awareness. This may lead to sexual mysticism. It is believed that the Feri tradition is accessible to any gender and sexuality and any type of sexual mysticism isn't restricted to homosexual expression.

Reclaiming Tradition

The Reclaiming Tradition of Wicca was mostly initiated by one witch named Starhawk who lived in the San Francisco Bay Area of California. Starhawk was trained to study as well Dianic Wicca and Feri, and the Reclaiming Tradition grew out of the series of classes in spirituality and witchcraft she taught alongside Diane Baker in 1980. Popularity of these classes was so great that Starhawk, Baker, and the students decided to create a coven to carry on the traditions they initiated. As the coven expanded and became more popular, it attracted other practitioners from across the United States and the world. The result was the establishment of witches' camps during summer for those interested in the emergence of the Reclaiming Tradition. These camps, which are now referred to as "Witch Camps" are held each year throughout The United States, Canada, and Europe.

Reclaiming Tradition Reclaiming Tradition has no specific gods or goddesses, and there are no any requirements for initiation or ceremonies. Instead, the tradition puts an focus on environmental and social accountability, political engagement and self-discovery, as well as creativity and self-reliance. Anyone who is a part of Reclaiming Tradition Reclaiming Tradition are encouraged to develop new rituals that typically involve chanting, breathing dancing, energy-raising and the creation of ecstatic states.

In the sense there is a chance that Reclaiming Tradition has a theology, Reclaiming Tradition has a theology that is based on the concepts and images that are associated with The Pentacle of Iron, the Pentacle of Pearl, and the Three Souls are the most significant. Pentacles are made up of 5 points each that represents a distinct idea as well as a different aspect. The five points of the Pentacle of Iron represent sex, self passion, pride and the power of. Pentacle of Pearl Pentacle of Pearl is the opposite to the Pentacle of Iron and its points symbolize love, law, wisdom the power of knowledge and wisdom. The five points on each pentacle also correspond to the five body parts which are the head, two hands as well as the feet. It is believed that the Three Souls concept holds that every person has an older Self and a Talking Self and a God Self/Deep. The Younger Self is the unconscious, the Talking Self lends an expression to the conscious mind while the Deep/God self represents the sacredness inside each of us. Although it is true that the Reclaiming Tradition does not mandate the existence of a particular god, many rituals call for either a Goddess or God. It is believed that the San Francisco Bay Area in particular is a frequent place to invoke two gods called Brigit as well as Lugh.

Reclaiming Tradition Reclaiming Tradition has a Mission Statement as well as a series of "Principles of Unity" that define the goal and principles that guide the tradition. Its Mission Statement reiterates the tradition's determination to bring about change and emphasizes the importance of ritual and magic to help its followers. Its Principles of Unity include the Charge of the Goddess, which is a passage that comes from British Traditional Wicca that was written by Doreen Valiente as well in affirmations of the dedication to the commitment of Reclaiming Tradition practitioners to the Earth and to magic, spirituality, the Divine and the diversity. Because Reclaiming Tradition is a nontraditional rite of initiation, Reclaiming Tradition does not have a standard ceremony for initiation Any witch who is in accordance in these Principles of Unity and practices magic in the Reclaiming style is an incarnation in Reclaiming Tradition. Reclaiming Tradition. In this way, Reclaiming Tradition practitioners may be members of a solitaries or coven.

Cochrane's Craft

Cochrane's Craft is frequently regarded as an ancient tradition that falls under the under the umbrella of Wicca despite the fact that the creator, Robert Cochrane, disassociated himself and his practices from Wicca. Cochrane said he was an ancestral witch, who was taught the art of the art of witchcraft by elder members of his own family though the authenticity of this claim has been widely disputated. The tradition was established by Cochrane in the year 1951, which was around the same time Gardnerian Wicca began to gain recognition.

The Cochrane's Craft believed in the existence of a Horned God as well as a

Triple Goddess, as many other followers of practices of Wicca. The Horned God symbolizes the underworld, time and fire. Also referred to in the form of the White Goddess, is a trinity of the three women or three daughters. The Cochrane's craft followers also believed in seven gods that were believed to be descendants of both God the Horned God or the Triple Goddess. Cochrane as well as Gardner believed in a god who was beyond the comprehension of humans. He described this as"the "Hidden goddess" as well as the "Truth."

Rituals of Cochrane's Craft were carried out in dark, hooded robes that were tied by a ritual cord. The participants used an urn, a stone along with a knife, as well as an oblique staff, known as"stang. "stang." Cochrane did not have an Book of Shadows, so rituals were often devised in a way that was creative and spontaneous.

The first coven of Cochrane's Craft is known as the Clan of Tubal Cain, created by Cochrane in the United Kingdom. The first initiates were Cochrane's wife Jane as well as Evan John Jones, who was appointed the chief magistrate in the Clan Tubal Cain following the death of Cochrane. Doreen Valiente Gardner's High Priestess was once co-member of the Cochrane's Craft but quit after Cochrane refused to stop from slamming Gardner as well as Gardnerian Wicca. Cochrane's Craft, the Clan of Tubal Cain and Cochrane's Craft as a whole largely disintegrated in 1966 after Cochrane's spouse Jane had filed for divorce. Cochrane was a suicide victim shortly afterwards.

Cochrane is a notable name for being the source of the term "Gardnerian." This name was initially meant as a pun however, it became popular and has become the standard name for this practice of Wicca.

1734 Tradition

Just before his death, Robert Cochrane began to write letters to an American, Joe Wilson, who was fascinated by witchcraft. Wilson established his 1734 Tradition as an American cochrane's craft offshoot. The

1734 Tradition shares many of the same characteristics as Cochrane's Craft and is enriched by Joe Wilson's studies and practices. The source of 1734 as a reference to the tradition is debated and some sources claim that the number was an original mystery invented by Cochrane which is solved and gives what the word "1734" means to the goddess as well as others claiming that it is derived from the ornamentation on a copper altar.

Trinitarian Wicca

Trinitarian Wicca is a relatively recent form of Wicca that is often called "Christian Wicca." The name itself is controversial with both Wiccans as well as Christians which resulted in the adoption that Trinitarian Wicca name in its place. Trinitarian Wicca was established in 1999 and draws inspiration from both Alexandrian as well as Dianic Wiccan traditions. It also draws inspiration from Ancient Christianity, the Qabalah and Gnosticism.

There are many similarities Trinitarian Wicca and Christianity begin through the notion of the holy trinity. Other than that, Trinitarian Wicca rejects Christian dogmas, patriarchy, as well as the concept of sin. They believe in a particular form of the trinity, which includes God as Father God Jesus Christ, as well as God the Mother and believe this as the real model of the Christian Holy Spirit. They affirm their faith in the trinity with Bible passages, which is distinctive among Wiccan beliefs. The majority of Wiccans do not adhere to the Bible. Trinitarian Wicca is also a feminist traditionthat focuses on what it regards as the denial of the feminine nature in God within the Bible. Similar to other Wiccan practices, Trinitarian Wiccans celebrate the four Greater Sabbats, the four Lesser Sabbats, and the Esbats. They also adhere to Wiccan Rede, rather than the Wiccan Rede, rather than the Bible as their code of morality.

Ros an Bucca

Ros the Bucca was a small group located in Cornwall that is often grouped under the umbrella of "Wicca." Similar to numerous Wiccan practices, the practitioners perform ritual magic and practice the principles that is a form of paganism that is rooted in continuously evolving pre-Christian practices. Ros an Bucca could be considered to be a an element of Wicca in that it is likely to be an identical group, that of the New Forest coven, that started Gerald Gardner and provided the basis for the development of the entire field of Wicca.

Ros an Bucca recognizes a one god, The Bucca, who is typically associated with weather, tides balance, as well as the resolution of opposing forces. The Bucca is regarded as an ethereal god with an "white spirit" also known as Bucca Gwidder and an "black spirit" which is also called Bucca Dhu. It is believed that the Bucca Gwidder symbolizes the energy of the sun and it is believed that the Bucca Dhu symbolizes darkness. The Bucca in all its forms is usually symbolized with the skull of a honed creature , with candles in between the horns symbolizing the absolute unity of all, along with the knowledge that comes from the coming together of opposing forces.

Cultus Sabbati

Cultus Sabbati, like Ros and Bucca is not necessarily an Wiccan practice, but frequently is a part of Wicca due to it's neopagan or United Kingdom origins.

Cultus Sabbati is a blend of ritual folk magic ritual magic, ceremonial magic, tools that are similar to those used in traditional Wicca and also an belief in the significance of dreams, a state of mind that is characterized by terms that are derived in Christianity or Luciferianism. Despite these terms however, the religion isn't Satanist or Judeo-Christian, it is a Neopagan. Similar to Wicca the religion claims to have the pre-Christian European history.

Rituals performed in Cultus Sabbati do not take an exact form and are not passed on through generations strict as they are in British Traditional Wicca. The practitioners believe it's inherent in rituals and spells to alter their appearance as time goes by and the divine guidance of the spirits comes through. The inspiration usually comes through dreams. Practitioners actively create dream states in which they are able to communicate with spirits.

Cultus Sabbati is one of the most secretive neopagan practices that could be considered to be part of Wicca. In contrast to other Wiccan traditions, where only a small portion of information is oathbound as well as in other Wiccan traditions where rituals and ceremonies are publically accessible, Cultus Sabbati is a strictly private tradition. Members who come to the group and request an initiation are rejected on the basis of the basis of. The new members are initiated upon invitation only. Practitioners believe that if spirits wish to see someone be initiated into Cultus Sabbati there is a way that is discovered. The majority of information regarding Cultus Sabbati is from an famous writer, Andrew D. Chumbley who published under the pseudonym Xoanon. If Cultus Sabbati could be thought of as having an open theology his books or writings represent the primary source.

Chapter 5: Practicing Wicca

Covens

Covens are among the most well-known Wiccan groups, in part because of the way in which the term has been circulating through popular culture. The word "coven" in the way it appears in TV and films may be inaccurate or not reflect Wiccan covens as they actually exist in real life. Simply put, a coven is an organization of witches that gather to perform rituals. The membership of a coven is limited and set. New members are not able to join the coven at any time and must instead be accepted by current members. The rituals that the coven holds generally are not open for the general public. Only members are allowed to attend. In certain covens, participation during rituals could be required.

In some religions covens are restricted in size, and the process of initiating them is lengthy. British Traditional Wicca, for instance, typically limit the number of coven members to 13. Once a coven is able to reach thirteen members the coven will "hive," or split to create an entirely new coven. British Traditional Wicca also places an emphasis on the lineage-based initiation to new members. Due to the high barriers to joining some covens, the members are extremely dedicated towards the craft. They usually stay within the same coven for many years and build close friendships with other coven members. Every member contributes their own creativity, energy and a keen awareness of rituals. This is another reason that there are times when participation may be required.

The coven members don't just practice Wicca in a coven-based setting. In a similar way to Christian practices covens can be thought of as a church, which is a community comprised of people who have the same beliefs and practices them together. People also attend worship on their own at home, in a church setting or in small groups outside of the church. This is also true for covens. Witches meet with coven members to participate in rituals, however, they aren't limited to coven-based practices. Witches that belong to covens also engage in an extensive solitary ritual as a key aspect of Wiccan faith.

Covens meet in celebration of Sabbats or Esbats. If covens are part of a tradition which is a celebration of both the Greater Sabbats and the Lesser Sabbats the group will be gathered for the entire eight. Covens that belong to customs that only celebrate the four or six Sabbats are only gathered to celebrate the Sabbats that they acknowledge. Sabbats are a serious time of ritual however they also serve as occasions for celebrations that are joyful, such as dancing, music food, and drinks.

There are numerous benefits having covens. The close relationships that form between members of the coven allow for the building of trust and intimacy that can be built in very the most unlikely of places. Practically speaking it is simpler to boost the energy required to perform rituals and spell work when working with a group of people. If the group has an increase in energy levels, the entire group will attain greater results and build closer ties with the gods. This is beneficial for the whole group and for each member. Covens also provide an environment that is safe for growth and spiritual expression and growth, as well as the help system provided by coven's other members. However covens are sometimes too cliquey or cause power struggles between members. This is among the reasons why covens should be cautious when it comes to bringing on new members, and one of the reasons why some covens are low. Self-aggrandizement is a detriment to self-awareness, spirituality, and coven growth. Additionally, a closed coven may become a dogma and forget the significance to creativity within Wicca. But, covens are essential and a vital element in Wiccan life.

Circles

A circle, when understood in the broadest sense, is an organization of witches that gather to perform Wiccan rituals. Circles may be inclusive, welcoming everyone but they can also be closed in part. Circles that are partially closed may invite new members only to certain rituals, while keeping others shut or have a brief rituals of initiation for new members to the group. Certain circles meet regularly as do covens, however participation is not as required like it is in covens. Others are extremely loose and can meet only at random times, during special occasions or when certain events require the need for a ritual. They are similar to covens because they gather to conduct rituals, however they differ from covens because they don't adhere to a set of rules which all members must adhere to. Certain commonality of belief systems is essential to ensure that the ritual is meaningful to the participants, however, circles typically do not require the practice of a particular pantheon, have no an orderly leadership structure and welcome members of every race and religion.

Certain traditions are more suited for circles than other. Reclaiming Tradition, for instance. Reclaiming Tradition, for example is an open traditionthat allows self-initiation and regularly holding public ceremonies. The rituals aren't necessarily open to all curious members of the general public, however they are accessible to any person who is a practitioner of Wicca who wishes to join in and are more open than the majority of Wiccan rituals. The rituals for initiation in British Traditional Wicca make it an exclusive group which is less likely hold circles.

Witches are part of both the coven as well as the circle. They could benefit from the close bonds and profound spiritual experiences they gain within the coven, in addition to the less formal rituals that are practiced by the circle. Additionally, because circles don't have a members that are fixed, witches may move around as their habits and experiences determine. A circle membership could be a means for witches to study other traditions, particularly in the event that they discover that the one they initially joined isn't as suitable for them.

The most significant advantages of a circular group, in contrast to covens, is the creativity and inclusion that a group that is constantly evolving creates. Because the rituals and participants within a circle are always changing, there's no time for stagnation and there is always growth. Since initiation rituals are a bit loose or not present and circles are more inclusive than covens. For many Wiccans crucial to their rituals and circles create the best environment for inclusion. However, the fluid and ever-changing members of Wiccan circles can prevent a tightly formed group from being created. This can hinder trust and intimacy that are necessary for deep spiritual experiences that can be experienced in covens. Thus circles are more suitable to rituals that don't require the close connection between the gods and the participants in the circle.

Solitary Practice

Solitary Wiccans perform magical tasks independently and aren't part of covens, though they might join the circle from time to time to take part in group rituals or take part in sessions on Wicca. Wiccans can have a variety of methods and draw on many different practices, including other religions and ideas. Wiccans tend to do solitary practices in various ways. Some start with solitaries, and do not join a coven. They discover that they're better practice alone. Some begin with a membership in a coven but then leave and practice solitary. Some are not solitary out of preference, but don't live in close proximity to covens or are unable to locate a coven that is compatible to their practices and beliefs. Every witch, including members of covens or regularly participate in circles and are sometimes associative. Wiccan practice doesn't end after the end of a ritual So every witch can connect with the gods as well as conduct rituals and gain spiritual growth in a solitary environment.

Certain traditions of Wicca are extremely suitable for an enclave, solo practice however others aren't. Traditions with oath-bound material like most British Traditional Wicca, are difficult to practice in solo practitioner because some of the rituals and rites are not accessible to studying. Additionally, those with a strict procedure or lineage to initiate are unable to be accepted without being a member of covens. Solitaries tend to follow more loosely-structured traditions like Seax-Wica, the Reclaiming Tradition or Seax-Wica. Some solitaries develop their own practices according to what is important to them. The idea for solitary practices could be derived from Wiccan texts, such as the Books of Shadows, fairy stories, folk witchcraft The Qabalah, Gnosticism, Tantra, Voodoo, Enochian Magic, Thelema, the Hermetic Order of the Golden Dawn, Sufism, Yezidism, Zoroastrianism and many more kinds of thought and theology. A lot of witches who played a role in the creation of various Wiccan practices began as solemnists looking for magical practices that were meaningful and useful for them, and then sharing these practices with others.

It is beneficial to practice alone because it is openand without dogmas, liturgy and the expectations of other people. Witches can worship their gods or gods according to what is most important for them. In the case of some people, it might be in the form of an a particular liturgy derived from the Book of Shadows. Others, the format of their worship could change every time. A single practice can allow for this flexibility and lets each witch decide what's best for her. It can also be an ideal choice for shy witches or those who are sensitive to the divine energy. The powerful energies that are generated by rituals in groups may overpower people who are sensitive. But, the smaller quantity of energy generated by solo practice could be a problem, since certain rituals or spells require more energy and the amount that is gathered often correlates with outcomes achieved. Another disadvantage of practicing solitary is that like all religions it is beneficial to form a community that allows for growth and spiritual development beyond what a single person could achieve by themselves. Solo witches might want to find an advisor in the event that they feel their development is stagnant. In any case the practice of solitary is a vital element of every Wiccan rituals. If you are a part of the coven or a circle make sure you don't let your solitary practices slip in the dust, since your spiritual growth is affected.

Chapter 6: Getting Started Your Wiccan Practice

If you're looking to become Wiccan there are numerous methods to begin to study witchcraft. A single practice is among the easiest methods by which you can start to figure out which Wiccan practice is best for you.

While it is easy and thrilling to dive right into magical rituals, such as making a circle or connecting to gods, it's crucial to conduct plenty of research before beginning any rituals or spells. Despite the secrecy surrounding certain Wiccan traditions, there's an abundance of information regarding various gods as well as the importance of magic and magic-related energies and the importance of enlightenment in Wicca. It is also important to be acquainted with the many Wiccan principles of morality, which includes Wiccan Rede, the Wiccan Rede, the Law of Threefold Return and the different interpretations of these ideas which are found in a few Wiccan practices. Although your views on morality and morality may change over time but it's always recommended to take a moment to reflect about the good and bad before beginning any type of magic-related practice. Magical acts are liable to consequences and you should be able to anticipate these consequences before you begin any actions.

Establishing a connection with a god or goddess is also essential prior to engaging in a ritual or magic practice. Although you could choose the god or goddess of an array and dedicate your time to them, you'll get better results if have built a strong relationship to the god. You might want to begin by studying the different gods that are revered by different religions of Wicca. Spend time in meditation and dedicate your thoughts to each god each one at a time. You may prefer to spread this out over several meditation sessions instead of all at all at. If you feel a strong connection to a particular god or god, try to further explore the connection by continuing your meditation sessions. You might find that you have a connection with several gods. Keep in mind that Wiccans may be monotheistic, duotheisticor pantheistic, polytheistic or atheist or any combination of these. If you notice that you have a connection with multiple gods, you could start to believe that they're all parts of a single god Or, you might discover that they are distinct entities that exist on their own. This process of exploration will allow you to select the right tradition, if you choose to follow it. Certain traditions have a particular pantheon, whereas others don't. You should pick one that allows you to keep calling to the gods or gods that you have established an affinity.

Studying the foundations of Wiccan rituals and texts and reflecting on morality and developing a relationship with gods or gods can be extremely beneficial when you begin the rituals and eventually, spellcasting. It also makes it much simpler for you to join a religion in the event that you decide to join one. One reason why some Wiccan groups of any kind are more secretive and exclusive is the fact that

Wicca's popularity or even popularity is sometimes attracted those who are more interested in the superficial value of the craft, not dedicated practice, spiritual growth and a sense of community. An in-depth investigation about Wicca and a close connection to the Divine will demonstrate to the people who belong to a particular tradition that you're truly keen to learn more about the Craft.

The next step to your practice is to begin to practice simple rituals. Solo rituals aren't as complicated as the rituals of circles or covens because one person is in the process. If you're new to magic it is possible that you don't have several or even a few of the tools employed in rituals. This is fine. Although magic tools are integral to many cultures however, they have gained their importance due to their use, and not because they have any particular meaning or significance as objects. This is why it is appropriate to utilize an item that you find meaningful in a spiritual perspective regardless of whether it's not an authentic Wiccan magical instrument. The best place to start is to make use of candles. You can select candles that reflect colours of each of the elements and they will be used to symbolize those four cardsinal directions as well as the center of your magic circle. As you begin to engage in rituals, you'll want to know more about how to build an altar. Like many other non-Wiccan religionsand practices, the altar is the main place of the worship as well as ritual. Altars in Wicca may take on a variety of different forms. When you're beginning out you should select an altar which is most important and meaningful for you. As you advance through your journey you'll be able to alter the altar that will help your altar serve your worship and draw divinities to holy space.

An excellent first step in beginning rituals is to understand how to cast circles. There are numerous guides available online and in numerous Wiccan books on how to cast circles. Check out a variety of them. You might be amazed at the things you can learn from them and how you can add from the techniques you find. Most importantly, Wicca is a process that allows you to discover yourself, your and your power, of your relationship with the gods as well as the community and how you can effect transformation. The process begins with a private practice, whether or not you choose to become a part of the tradition or you continue to be an individual. Begin to understand the potential of the Craft when you begin to learn rituals, and eventually make spells.

It is possible that you have started your studies and practices with the intention of joining a particular tradition or realize that your practice could benefit from more formal gathering with other witches. Joining an established tradition is simple or extremely difficult, according to where you're situated and the tradition you'd like to join. Some traditions, like Ros an Bucca, are highly localized and don't have covens outside their region of origin. Other traditions, like Cultus Sabbati, are not able to accept the request for an initiation. The practices that are part of British

Traditional Wicca require a procedure for joining, however, their practices are widely practiced and covens are easy to locate. Certain Wiccan traditions originated and are mostly located in the West Coast of the United States. If you reside in another state, it could be difficult to locate covens. Certain traditions have extremely loose guidelines regarding the process of getting into the religion and you might, with enough research and practice you will be able to find a coven within your local area. An excellent place to start would be to Google search the city name (or the city closest to it that is the largest) as well as "Wicca." It is likely to reveal many Wiccan and neopagan groups. Another option is local shops for pagans. They can be asked whether they are aware of the local group. This is particularly helpful for those looking to learn more about British Traditional Wicca, which is more hidden. It is possible that you will have to give your contact details, since these groups do not share their contact information in a public manner. In certain cases covens can organize "outer courts" or "outer groves" gatherings that people who are not initiated attend to gain an understanding of what it means to be a part of a long-standing tradition.

If you've got more details about the options available in your local area If you are interested, do some exploration, talk to members, join open circles or gatherings, and decide which group is right for you. Certain groups are open for anyone who is interested in joining and some are either closed or accepting applicants only through an interview. Be mindful of the coven's rules on new members. Like any other religious or spiritual practices, Wicca is a highly personal belief system. covens seek to shield their members from the negative influences. If your motives and beliefs are pure, participants of your coven recognize it by the help of spirits. If a coven rejects your admission Do not take it personally Most likely, the spirits suggested that you weren't ready to join yet or you were not the best person for the coven. Keep searching, and you'll find a coven that is a good fit for you.

It's possible that chances to participate in Wiccan practicing in a circle or coven environment are very few and far between in your region or even with your own effort and efforts, you can't locate a group an ideal fit to you. If this is the case, technology will help you locate an internet-based Wiccan community. There are some covens which exist solely online. Also, using a Google search can be a good start to find an online coven. However, be sure to ensure that the group you join is genuine. Just like any other location online, individuals aren't always who claims to be and things might not be as they appear. Keep in touch with the principles and values you believe to be true and, if you begin to feel like the coven you've joined does not reflect those values anymore then it could be an appropriate time to leave. This is true for covens that are physically located, not only virtual ones!

If you belong to an organization that is affiliated with British Traditional Wicca, or one that has rituals for initiation, the experiences after being accepted as a coven member can be different and could vary. As discussed in chapters 3 and 4 Certain traditions use the initiation process in three steps however others only require only one step. The rituals used in the process of initiation differ between covens, and some initiates have to take a course of study. This is especially the case for covens with Oathbound materials, which be available to new initiates after they have completed at the very least the first level of init. Some covens also provide challenging to the initiates. These challenges are designed to be challenging however, they are not impossible and to foster personal growth for the initiate. Whatever the path, be prepared for the process of initiation to be challenging. Initiation into the world of Wicca and the gods of the past isn't granted to anyone. You might feel incredibly happy with the way you've done it when you've completed the ceremony of initiation, but remember your personal and spiritual growth is never finished for those who are a practitioner of Wicca.

Chapter 7: History Of The Use Of Oils

The aromatic oils as they've been referred to for centuries were used by different cultures around the world over the course of hundreds of years. Their applications varied from one religion, from healing to rituals of religious significance. It's hard to pinpoint exactly the essential oil was first discovered to have healing properties however this information quickly became widely known, and essential oils began to gain prominence.

The first evidence that can be traced of the use of herbs to treat ailments was found in Lascaux which is located in part of the Dordogne, France region. The cave paintings in the Paleolithic period demonstrate that they utilized herbs for healing in their daily life. The carbon dating dates this back to the year 18,000 BCE.

Egypt

The history of the record has revealed that Egyptians made use of essential oils in the year 4500 BCE. They were renowned for their knowledge of the use of essential oils and ointments and cosmetology. Their most well-known formulation for herbs was called Kyphi it contained 16 ingredients that they could use for an aromatherapy as medicine, incense, or perfume.

They used aromatic types of vinegar or spices, resins, fragrant barks fragranced oils as well as Balsams in their daily life. The oils and pastes they extracted in plants would be used to create Ointments, suppositories and powders for medicinal use and even pills.

Watermelon ashes and smoke as well as grapes, garlic onion, cedar and aniseed, among others, were also used. In the time that Egypt reached its peak of power it was the priests who were the only individuals who could make use of aromatic oils. They were viewed as necessary to achieve union with Gods.

Every god was given their own scent The worshippers would then anoint their idols with the scent's oil. The Pharaohs even made their own blends of meditation, love, war and so on.

Gums such as myrrh and cedar were used for embalming and to preserve bodies, and evidence of these plants have been found on old Mummies. Although essential oils were extremely important in Ancient Egypt but they didn't begin to make their own and were only available oil from cypress and cedar.

China

The first documented oil use in China was in the period 2697 - 2597 BCE under the Huang Ti reign who was the famous Yellow Emperor. He wrote The Yellow Emperor's Book of Internal Medicine that contained applications for various essential oils. It's regarded as the classic essential oil book among today's Wicca fans.

India

The old-fashioned Indian medicine, also known as Ayurveda has been used to make essential oils to make curative concoctions over the last 3000 years. Vedic literature includes more than 700 compounds that include myrrh, sandalwood as well as ginger, cinnamon and as vital in healing.

Ayurveda was used successfully in its use in the Bubonic Plague outbreak to provide an alternative to antibiotics that failed to perform. They didn't consider aromatic oils or plants as merely medicines and believed that they were an essential part of the human experience as a whole, and this played significant roles in how they perceived Ayurvedic medical practices both spiritually and philosophically.

Greece

The Greeks kept the records of their oil-related information that they acquired from the Egyptians about 400-500 BCE. Myrrhool was an essential ingredient for soldiers in combat to fight diseases.

Hypocrites The Greek doctor who lived between 377 and 460 BCE was now referred to for being called the Father of Medicine. He wrote down the effects of more than 300 plants, including marjoram, cumin, peppermint, the thyme and saffron.

The knowledge Hypocrites received about the spirits of plants and plants were closely related to Ayurvedic. This information was discovered by the Greek soldiers came across Ayurvedic treatment in India when they traveled together with Alexander the Great. They soon realized that Ayurveda was compatible alongside their own healing practices. You can still see the mingling of these two practices in tribal communities that are remote today.

Hypocrites taught his fellow Greek people that the best method to maintain good health was to get a fragrant massage and bath daily. The entire books that Hypocrites and his students created are extremely beneficial to the current medical practices. The primary goal of a doctor is to stimulate a patient's natural healing. It is evident the impact that Hypocrites has played on the field of modern medicine in a variety of areas, but most notably with respect to the Hippocratic Oath they all doctors adhere to.

Galen is a different famous Greek with a vast knowledge of plants and their therapeutic uses have had an enormous influence on the way things are classified in the present. He started his education as a surgeon at an academy for gladiators. They said that during the time Galen was a doctor and no gladiator suffered a fatal injury. There was a buzz about his skills and soon he was appointed personal physician to his Emperor Marcus Aurelius. He published a large portion of his theories on the medicinal properties of plants and classified them into various categories, which are still referred to as Galenic.

Rome

Romans enjoyed applying essential oils to their clothing, bedding and even their bodies. They also used oils for their massages and baths. In the time of their fall from Rome the doctors were forced to take all their books from Hypocrites or Galen. The books were transliterated to Persian, Arabic, and various other languages.

Persia

Avicenna the Arab Also called Ali-Ibn Sana was born in 980 to 1037 AD and was regarded as to be a child prodigy as well as an educated physician at twelve years old. He then wrote an article that described the effects that the 800 plants were able to have on the human body. He was regarded as the first to learn and record the method of distilling essential oils. The methods are still in use to this day.

Europe

Their armies of knights absorbed herbalism knowledge they acquired during The Middle East and Western Europe during the Crusades. They knew how to distill and take the oil that smelled perfumed along.

The 14th century was during the midst of the Bubonic Plague, people used to burn frankincense and pine throughout the major routes to ward off evil spirits. There were less deaths in these regions in comparison to those where they didn't burn the herb.

Nicholas Culpeper wrote The Complete Herbal in 1653 which is still an important source of information today. The book outlines a variety of ailments and ways to treat them. This book continues to function today.

Rene-Maurice Gattefosse, a French Chemist, invented the term Aromatherapie as he studied the way essential oils might be utilized to treat antiseptic issues. He published his book Aromatherapie around 1928. In the book , he explained the characteristics of various essential oils. His work had a huge effect upon French medicine.

In the event of an explosion in his laboratory the scientist was able find lavender's healing properties. The hands of one was severely burned. He put his injured hand into the liquid close to his hand. The lavender oil was the liquid, and to his delight the hand that was burned healed without wounds or scars.

Gattefosse together with many of his colleagues continued to study all of lavender's properties and then would transport lavender to various institutions in France. There was no death of hospital staff during Spanish influenza because of the usage of lavender.

The use of Oils in Magic

Our ancestors used oil in ceremonies and rituals during their lives. They made use of essential oils and they are accessible today. We can even make our today.

They made it happen by adding flowers and herbs to the fat or oil while it was heated. To use it in the realm of magic, it's recommended to make use of essential oils. They are more powerful and have magical properties. This makes your spells more powerful and efficient.

There are a variety of ways to utilize oils in rituals. They're extremely versatile and can be applied to altar equipment, Wiccan jewelry, necklaces or amulets as well as candles. The powerful energy of the oil are infused with the magical symbolism and the properties of the tools that are used.

The oil can be used to apply an oil on your body. Essential oils are extremely concentrated and may cause allergic reactions in certain individuals. Make sure to use them in moderation. Mix them with carrier or base oil to reduce their concentration.

Applying the oil to your body, it will attract the positive energy that the oils have to offer. If you rub money-drawing oil onto your body, you will attract cash and love.

Amulets, charms, talismans and crystals that are infused with oils can give the illusion of power and magic. They use the oil to ensure your wishes come true.

Essential oils, aromatic oils condition oil and ritual oils, as well as herbal essential oils, and spiritual oil are extensively utilized to support Paganism as well as Witchcraft. They are used for life-changing occasions, rituals or ceremonies, as well as in events which commemorate times that bring change throughout the year. They are available in a variety of types of flavors, colors, and colors and it isn't easy choosing which oil to use.

Each oil has a symbolism that can enhance the effect of the spell-casting or ritual. Oils are a symbol of Spirit. They aid in taking us into a new dimension and call out to the spirits who we wish to communicate with. Here are a few types of oils:

The Ritual Oils are: They oils are employed to anoint cash furniture, furniture, altar instruments as well as candles, ritual tools and many other items.

Anointing Oils can be used for anointing the body.

* Lucky Hoodoo, Conjure Condition Oils: These refer to the dressing oils and anointing oils which are used by people who adhere to an African American folk path in the spell-craft, rituals and rituals to deal with any unwelcome condition or create the desired state.

The oils are used for aromatherapy. They can be used to treat ailments in the past by ancient Chinese, Romans, Persians, Greeks, and Egyptians. They are used in healing, cosmetics skin care, massages and baths.

* Essential oils These are essential oils which contain the scent of the plant they come from. They are used to create fragrances or flavorings and can be combined with base oils to intensify a number of blends of oils.

- Synthetic fragrance oils: They are produced in a lab to make them smell like flowers or natural herbs which they're named after. These should not be used for rituals or magic since they have no magic or symbolic power.

* Hand-crafted or herbal oils The blends are made for particular ritual or magical purpose. They are made up of real herbs that are blended with base oils. They are hand-crafted and blessed with the principles that are part of Hoodoo rituals or Witchcraft customs.

Biology and Scent

Scents can help you go to sleep, get you up, increase attraction or reduce stress. This article will explain what scents be different in their effects on your well-being.

The scents of flowers that are applied to a bedroom prior to going to bed could result in better sleep than any smells at all or unpleasant smells.

While the scents of our bedtimes affect the dreams we experience the actual smells are found included in less than one of 100 dreams. We have dreams about our daily worries like shopping, sports or driving with friends.

Our smell may not be like animals however it is a crucial factor in our physical and mental well-being and emotional.

It is believed that the effects smell has on the brain stem go back to the death and life circumstances that smell triggered on the early man. The smell cells are connected with the limbic system, which has the longest-running brain part which controls the long term memory of behavior and emotional state.

The sense of smell in us is controlled by us, and in the early days of man, this sense was much more potent and allowed him to detect both of his enemies and food. Although the sense of survival is mostly gone however, its effects on the body as well as brain persist.

Research has proven that scent can affect everything, including memory, romance as well as pain, concentration gambling, stress, driving, and emotional states. The scent of lavender releases feel-good hormones and make us feel content. The aroma of roses may reduce blood pressure. Eucalyptus can help increase alertness.

The smell of a scent can also influence the amount we spend, the things we purchase or even how to play. A study that was conducted in a casino revealed the presence of a fifty percent increase in the amount of money gambled after a pleasant smell was applied to the machines. The study found an 84-percent increase in people who bought shoes found them to be more attractive when they were placed in a room where the air was sprayed with pleasant scent as when compared to the same pair in a room that was not sprayed with a scent.

For more positive and positive dreams, smell flowers before heading to the bed. Both men and women with a smell of hydrogen sulfide, flowers or no scent at the research center found that the quality of their dreams was related to the smell they experienced. People with an aroma that was pleasant were more relaxed in their dreams when compared to those with no smell or who were exposed to the scent of Sulphur suffer from nightmares. Researchers are currently looking to determine if pleasant scents will decrease the likelihood of having nightmares.

Vanilla, coffee and lavender are all able to aid in reducing stress and insomnia. Studies have proven that lavender is a great remedy for post-operative pain, stress, insomnia, and anxiety. There is evidence to suggest that lavender aromatherapy can slow the activities of the nervous system, improves mood improves relaxation and improves the quality of sleep for people suffering from sleep disorders.

Coffee smell can cause feeling more calm. Vanilla has a soothing effect while roses lower breathing and blood pressure.

Lavender, strawberry and peppermint are great for concentration. Spraying lavender in breaks at the Japan factory increased the post-break productivity. The athletes who smelled the peppermint scent had more focus and were faster. Children performed better in tests when exposed to the scent of strawberries.

The smells trigger specific memories . They can be used to retrieve lost memories. Memory triggers that are activated by smells can be more emotionally charged, vivid, and more clear. The part of the brain that responsible for processing smells is connected to the brain that controls emotions and memory.

The smell of a person can affect their feelings for someone else. Women are able to detect genetic differences. Women love the smells of those with distinct genetic material that is associated with immunity. This is due to the fact that mating with the person can result in offspring that have an immune system that is stronger.

The Cost of Purchasing Oils

Essential oils are concentrated versions of volatile compounds that naturally occur in plants that are aromatic. If you've had the pleasure of smelling your hands after you had rubbed the lemon between your hands, you may have taken a whiff of essential oils released as your hands broke the oil glands inside the peel.

It is possible to smell the aromas of rosemary, orange oil and peppermint whenever you go about your business because only one tiny drop to let out its distinctive scent. It takes a lot of raw materials and a precise extraction to extract just an ounce worth of essential oil. This is evident in the cost.

There are many different methods by which oil can be extracted:

Cold Pressed: The plants that release their components quickly can be cold-pressed in order to get their oil. This technique was employed in the past to extract citrus oils from the skins of their fruits. Manual extraction involves pressing the fruit using the help of a sponge. The sponge will be saturated with oil. These sponges would then be pressed to extract the oil. The process has now been automated so that the oil can be removed from the mixture of oil-juice which is derived.

The aroma of cold-pressed oils is fresh and have a light color. The raw materials aren't exposed to heat, so they retain the same aroma as the plant in its original form. They are considered to be the finest essential oils available for this reason. This process isn't appropriate for the extraction of most all essential oils.

Steam extracted steam is passed over the substance which is sealed in a vessel. The oil gets vaporized , and increases with steam. The steam then flows through a vent to the chamber of condensation. Both the water and aromatic vapor turn to liquid in this chamber however they are separated into distinct layers due to their capacity to be separated.

A lot of essential oils weigh less than water, which is why they make up the upper layer and be easily sucked away. Clove oil is an one exception to this. Clove oil is much heavier, and so it forms at the bottom.

Essential oils extracted from the bark, roots as well as flowers and leaves of plants are usually steam-distilled. Eucalyptus oils sandalwood, peppermint and lavender are all extracted in this manner. While the raw materials are heated in the steam process but the essential components aren't elevated to a temperature of which is over that of the water's boiling point. Steam distillation essential oils are the most superior alternative to cold-pressed oils.

Solvent extraction: This is a chemical procedure in which the use of a solvent for binding to the changeable oils contained in the raw substances. The solvent is then separated from the mixture and is then transformed into the final product known as absolute. Alcohol is the solvent of choice in the majority of extraction processes for essential oils because it is easy to obtain. It is easily evaporated leaving behind pure oil.

Modern industrial processes make use of various organic compounds that can be changed, including propane, hexane, and Acetone. The likelihood for these substances leaving harmful residues in their wake generally casts doubt on their security. These chemicals are not utilized for therapeutic purposes.

There is no such thing as therapeutic quality oils. There are numerous products that advertise with this label. It is important to determine the quality essential oil you're looking for to use in a therapeutic way. Don't look for a label that holds no significance; you have to ask these questions when searching to purchase essential oils

1. Are they pure? The first thing to be looking for is quality. There are many oils available. Certain are developed and sold by trusted businesses. In the event that you've got specific goal in mind, and you discover a suitable blend, it can save you from buying various oils and then make the mix yourself.

However Don't think that just because one mix is effective for one person, it's the same for everyone else. Each person has their own body composition and each person reacts to the same ingredients in a different manner. It is impossible to confirm every ingredient or the properties of blended oils.

Buy pure oils on a per-item basis Even if only you have the money for just a tiny amount. They're extremely concentrated, which means that a small amount goes a long ways. It is possible to determine whether something is working for you or if might experience negative reactions.

2. Are they organic? It is also crucial to take into consideration when buying essential oils that can be used for therapeutic purposes. These are highly concentrated plant essences and it is possible that there is pesticide residues within the oil. If it is present the presence of pesticides, they will be than magnified. Search for oils taken from crops organically grown. If you can look for oils that have an appropriate certification.

There are times when essential oils are extracted from plants taken in the wild rather than cultivable plants. It may not be possible to obtain a certification for these oils. They could still be natural and could be more organic than products that have been certified. You can be sure that they are secure if you are confident in the seller.

3. Do I really need this? There are several different variations of the same oil, all of which are certified organic and 100% pure. They may not be the way you imagine them to be.

Oils can be extracted from plants with similar names. For instance, chamomile. There's Roman in addition to German chamomile. They aren't even related. Their properties and therapeutic benefits are completely different, as well.

They can be distinguished by their color. German Chamomile is a vivid blue. The Roman is a light yellow. This isn't the case for other oils.

Check that you know the Latin name is mentioned alongside the common name.

Essential oils that have a close relationship to a species may create confusion, just like numerous citrus plants. Orange oil is extracted from various varieties of oranges. Sweet orange oil is derived from Citrus sinensis, while bitter orange oil is derived out of Citrus aurantium. You can trust Citrus aurantium, the Latin name.

Certain oils come from various components from the exact same source. This can be quite confusing. The oil taken from freshly cut ginger is completely different from the oil made from dried ginger. Aromatically and therapeutically, Cinnamon spice is extracted directly from the wood of the plant, as is its essential oil. The leaves produce a completely distinct oil with distinct flavor and aroma.

Citrus aurantium fruit produces bitter orange oil, however there are two additional essential oils you can get through the same tree. Neroli is derived directly from flowers. Petitgrain is extracted from leaves. The names they are commonly used for would be useful in this instance.

Always verify whether the part of the plant is listed on the packaging.

4. Does the company have credibility? The most important aspect here is the credibility of the firm that manufactures vital oils. It's nearly impossible to know the

purity of the oil. The best thing you can do is to find an authentic source.

Avoid firms that sell a wide range of types of oil at the same time. Beware of bargains which appear too appealing to be true. Find other aromatherapists and people who utilize essential oils.

Synthetics

Synthetics are less expensive to produce and are easier to use and can be used to produce a greater variety of scents. But is the cost worth the cost? Let's see.

It is not clear the extent to which synthetic fragrances are ubiquitous and yet, we come into daily contact with them. Cleaning and laundry products such as perfumes, colognes air fresheners, and lots of household and personal care products contain synthetic fragrances created in labs using petroleum as well as a variety of chemicals. They are generally not extremely healthy. These scents attempt to replicate the natural scent of essential oils, but at the lowest price. This is the primary reason why people prefer these scents.

They are available more easily and are more widely available as essential oils. Essential oils are typically available in specific grocery stores as well as online, health-food stores and even aromatherapy shops. Synthetic oils can create various scents and make new scents which natural oils aren't able to. What is the Hawaiian scent?

Preservatives are present in these products, which means they will last for a long time. This makes them simple to store and you are able to use them when you require. You can save money because you won't have to purchase fresh ones when you don't need often. The smell will last longer and lasts longer. This means you will make use of less and you'll get exactly the same fragrance, feel and viscosity every time.

With all these benefits but there are also disadvantages. Although you could make use of these products for a long time without a problem but you must be aware that synthetic oils could be contaminated with certain contaminants. Parabens, sulfates and sulfates are among the glycol, benzyl alcohol, and benzaldehyde are just several. There are many dozen common chemicals used that are found in the products. Around 95 percent are derived via petroleum byproducts.

Mineral oil and petroleum jelly are both by-products from petroleum. They aren't naturally occurring or organic and should not be utilized in aromatherapy. Mineral oil is commonly used in baby oils and other moisturizers because it's a cheap oil to produce. Petroleum jelly and it can block pores, preventing your skin's ability to breathe, stop toxic substances from leaving the body through sweat, and prevent essential oils from being absorbed and can be used by the body to hinder the utilization of vitamins effectively within the body.

Companies that produce synthetic fragrances must add toxic solvents in order that their scents do not disperse into the air. They also add harmful chemical compounds to create molecules of fragrance sticky, and they adhere to furniture, skin hair, clothing and other surfaces. The scent can last for months, days or even hours. The result is a more lasting scent, but it is accompanied by harmful chemicals.

Fakes

It is quite simple. However, finding a good one can be a difficult task even for a trained aromatherapist. It is the bottle of potent oil that is distilled from the leaf, rind or flower of any plant that has aromatic properties.

Unfortunately, it's difficult to figure out what's inside the bottle you bought. Some companies make the oil more potent using it in combination with lower-cost oil from seeds and nuts. Some even pass cheap oils as those that aren't available. Others fake with synthetics that imitate the scent of the plant.

Here's how to identify the best stuff:

This is a fun fact to know that essential oils aren't real oils. They were given that term because they do not play with water. This small niggle can be useful when you are looking for any hidden seeds, vegetable or nut oils that may have been hidden in the primary oil. How do you test this? Apply a drop of oil onto white printer paper and let drying. If it creates an oily ring, it's not an essential pure oil. This is a drawback because some oils are stronger and darker in color, such as patchesouli German Chamomile, Vetiver and sandalwood.

Price doesn't always mean high quality. It's a good idea to stay clear of essential oil with an extremely low price. Essential oils can be expensive. It requires a large space of plants to create one tiny bottles of essential oils. When the plants are not readily available and expensive, the price will be more expensive. Certain oils like the sweet-smelling oranges, rosemary and lavender are readily accessible that they are always excellent. There are varieties of chamomile that include helichrysum, lemon balm, jasmine and rose are quite expensive. Find different websites to see the various costs.

Check that it is the Latin name is displayed in the product's label. If you're shopping on the internet, ensure they provide it on their site. If the name for lavender essential oil appears given as an option, you could be paying for something that is a hybrid. If it does not say the essential oil it likely isn't. Lavender is nothing more than an oil that smells. It may or may not contain any plant material, and does not possess the same healing properties like the genuine essential lavender oil.

Essential oils must be stored in glass containers. The strong chemical compound of oils disintegrates and will react with the plastic. Glass must be dark blue or amber to shield it from UV radiation. Check the temperature you place it at. Bottles should be kept in a cool location as temperatures can alter the chemical composition of oil.

Put a drop of seeds, nut or plant oil, on the pads of an index finger. Then, place a drop of vital oil onto the opposite. Rub the oils on your fingertips. Note any differences in the way they feel. Essential oils are known to have a tiny amounts of slip, however they shouldn't feel oily or heavy. Rich, heavy colored oils such as patchouli

German chamomile, vetiver and sandalwood are some exceptions.

When you remove the cap off an vital oil must be sealed by the aid of an orifice reduction device. This is a device that determines the quantity of drops you can pour out at a time. This can help get the right dosage, however it also extends shelf-life by limiting exposed to the air. It's not the end of the world if the bottle doesn't contain a dropper, but look out for essential oils that come with droppers. The tubes are made from plastic or rubber and may be broken down and let out impurities into the oil.

Essential oils come from plants, so the idea of avoiding pesticides by purchasing only organic oils is sensible. The majority of companies carry their own officially recognized USDA seal, however there is a secret that oils that are labeled wild-crafted are also safe. This simply means that the plant was grown in the wild , not raised for cultivation. It is safe to say they aren't spray-treated. Organic labels will result an increase in cost, so be cautious in deciding whether you'd prefer to save money or go overboard. Be sure to purchase natural citrus oils. They usually contain pesticides.

Storing

If you preserve your essential oils properly they should last at least one year. There are a few things that can influence your oils:

* Heat and light Essential oils are flame-proof. Every oil has its own flashpoint. The flashpoints are typically extremely high. The normal temperature of a room is good. Avoid storing oils on the stove or on the range. Sunlight exposure can also alter the colour of the oil as well as its constituents. The storage of them near or on a window is not recommended .

* Oxygen and Moisture The process of oxidation occurs when oils are exposed to oxygen. The constant contact with air degrades the oil, and can increase the rate of evaporation. There is no loss in the event of this happening. Oil can be used to clean products, but do not use it for therapeutic purposes and avoid contact

with the skin. Moisture can also damage the oil bottle. It could get into an oil reservoir if the lid has been not removed from the container for a long time. If water seeps in the oil it can be cloudy, or the water could end up dripping up at the surface of the vessel.

Here are some storage suggestions to store your oil:

To shield your oils from heat and light, keep them in the bathroom or kitchen cabinet. It's basically any area where there isn't sunlight.

Amber or cobalt bottles are more appealing than clear glass. They are usually in a colored bottle however, if you happen to find one, are not, don't attempt to change the bottle. Don't put the bottles in plastic. They're corrosive, and they'll cause the container to break.

Make sure to cover the bottle when not in use to prevent humidity and oxidation. It is recommended to transfer oil from a bottle that's almost completely empty, to a small bottle. If you are using a lot of essential oils and purchase the oil in 4-ounce portions then transfer the oil to smaller bottles after you've used up at minimum half the oil. The smaller space you can have in the bottle the more efficient.

A lot of half-ounce or one-ounce bottles come with a reducer cap attached to the cap. They allow you to dispensing oil by dropping a drop at a time. They're made of durable plastics and do not come into contact with the oil while they are not in use.

Certain oils are too heavy to fit in the caps of reducers or don't have one. This is when glass droppers can prove useful. Make sure to not make use of the dropper as lids for bottles. The bulb of the dropper are composed of rubber and can be destroyed if used for lids. Make sure you make use of your screw lid included with the bottle to store the bottles. The dropper can be cleaned using alcohol in the future for storage or use and storage. You can also create a specific dropper to be used with certain oils.

If you follow these guidelines, you will guarantee that your oils will last for as long as you'll need them.

Chapter 8: The Most Powerful Oils

We've discussed the advantages of essential oils and the various ways that they can assist in helping help the body heal itself. In this article, we will discuss the most potent oils and what they can do for you.

Ylang-Ylang

Prolific is the word that is in my mind when I think of Ylang Ylang. Ylang Ylang kills depression. It is the oldest-known health benefit that is Ylang Ylang. It can combat depression, and aids in relaxing and calm the mind and body. It can have a positive affect on mood and bring feelings of optimism and joy.

It is employed to treat a variety of infections. Every abrasion, burn or cut is at possibility of infection. This is especially true in the event that the wound was caused from an iron object, which carries the possibility of contracting Tetanus. The essential oil from Ylang Ylang can help to keep infections at bay if you employ it to disinfect your skin since it stops the development of microbes. It helps to recover faster too.

Seborrhoeic Eczema is a horrible condition that is caused by sebaceous glands malfunctioning, causing an infection of epidermal cells. The skin appears pale yellow or white dry, oily, or dry and eventually, it begins to peel where there is hair. Ylang Ylang essential oil can help in curing inflammation and helps reduce itching of skin due to increasing the production of sebum. It also treats the skin infection.

This essential oil may help bring back the sexual energy of couples who have lots of stress because of stress at work, family, or. Ylang Ylang is a great drug to lower blood pressure. The blood pressure medication that are prescribed may have extremely serious negative side negative effects. The oil is safe, natural and doesn't have any adverse negative effects when taken according to the directions.

It can soothe nerves. It helps alleviate the symptoms of panic attacks and anxiety and help to in calming and relaxing the patient.

Other advantages of ylang ylang include aiding in curing ailments of internal organs, such as colon, urinary tracts, stomach and intestines. It also helps with the effects of stress, such as frigidity as well as insomnia, fatigue, and frigidity. It assists in maintaining the moisture balance and oil balance of the skin and take good care.

Vetiver

Every living thing living on Earth utilize life energy, which is known as prana, and the essence is called the ojas. The plants use the same prana and ojas that come from the soil to transform into essential oils, food and medications that other living organisms can make use of.

From all the different varieties of plants in the universe the most potent option to capture all the subtleties of earthy scent is Vetiver.

In India the country, it is referred to as Khus and has evolved from a cooling herb to become an essential ingredient in a myriad of perfumes. It's also the foundation for these advancements in its incredible medicinal benefits which are lauded in the field of medicine.

Based on their beliefs the human body is composed out of 3 distinct doshas. One of them will be dominant and determines the character and character of a person. They three doshas are Kapha, Pitta, and Vata.

A deficiency in any of these could result in illness, and it indicates how the body's functions are not in equilibrium. Vata imbalances can trigger anxiety and restlessness, constipation dry skin and fever, as well as loss of memory and sleepiness. Pitta imbalances can cause skin irritation, jealousy, heartburn, ulcers, displeasure as well as high blood pressure and anger. Kapha imbalance is the cause of weight gain, slow digestion, constipation and a sluggish attitude.

The long-standing practices and medicinal benefits of the essential oil have become a crucial component of the Ayurvedic as well as Abhyanga massage therapies that help strengthen the nervous system, helps to combat stress and exhaustion as well as calms nerves and calms the mind.

Rose

The oil of rose, also is known as the fragrance of Venus can help ease the mood swings that occur during pregnancy and helps mothers during birth. What is the most beautiful way to welcome a baby to the world? Rose oil can also help alleviate the stress that occurs following the birth of a child.

Rose oil can also be employed as a companion for those who are dying. It eases fears and provides insight to those traveling to the other side.

Rose oil is known to have a strong psychological effect, even at very low concentrations. A couple of drops of the oil lamp can change the mood of a space.

Peppermint

Peppermint oil is a great item to keep in your bag. It's a potent oil that can be used for a variety of items, from energy boosts to digestive problems.

Here's a list of uses of essential oils from peppermint:

Apply drops of oil on your feet. Repeat this to ease fevers.

* Apply a drop to the temples to relieve headaches.

* Massage the stomach or inhale in order to reduce nausea.

Drop a drop of it under the nose or breathe in to boost your energy levels or to boost your alertness. Also, it can be added to diffusers to achieve the same outcomes.

* Place several drops of the spray bottle and spray it on your skin before going running or perform a vigorous exercise to keep you cool during hot days.

* Apply a few drops to the abdomen, focusing on the navel to help with indigestion.

Patchouli

The herb's fragrant and tender flavor features white flowers and soft oval leaves and upright stems. The leaves placed between clothes can deter insects. They give Indian Shawls the scent. Patchouli is the smell of India ink as well as Chinese the red paste of ink. Patchouli is a female.

It is believed to be associated to Osain, Pan, and Aphrodite. The astrological signification is Scorpio. It is ruled by the element earth as well as Saturn, the sun. Saturn.

This is because it is the component which is most frequently used. Patchouli has a scent similar to the earthy scent and is used in mixtures of money and prosperity and spells. The powder can be sprinkled onto money, arranged around the base of candles made of green and added into purses and wallets to increase prosperity. Patchouli is used to create fertility talismans and is able to be used in place of graveyard dust. It is a great addition to baths or love sachets. It can be used to draw people and encourage the desire to love. Incense is burned to attract fertility, money defense, protection passion, love, underworld, earth as well as releasing and removing. It is also used as aromatherapy for stress-related disorders such as nervous exhaustion, frigidity wrinkles, cuts, oily hair and skin as well as for impetigo, sores, hair treatment, fungal infections, eczema, dermatitisand dandruff chapped skin, broken skin, athlete's feet, and acne.

Its main characteristics are that it acts as a stimulant in small quantities. It acts as a sedative in large amounts. It can also serve as a nerve tonic as an aphrodisiac and arousing agent, for and relaxing.

Patchouli is widely used during Pagan rituals. Its exotic aroma brings a person back to exotic, far-off places and is often used for rituals involving incense blended, potpourri, and blends. It's an element of mint's family. The oils and leaves that are essential to its health, as well as the dried ones are among the most widely utilized parts. Certain practitioners also used the stems as well. The bush can grow up to 3 feet tall once fully mature. It's covered with white, purplish flowers. Patchouli oil is very strong. It has a rich musky, sour scent.

In certain hoodoo practices in some hoodoo traditions, a dollar symbol can be written on the paper using patchouli oil, and then carried around inside your wallet to bring money towards you.

There's a modern form of magic that uses patchouli for its power to repel. Put it in the doors and windows with oil or leaves to keep from negative influences or to create an enchanted self-defense.

It can be utilized in mixtures to provide love, protection or other qualities.

Palmarosa

The oil Palmarosa is a part of rose oil. It's a tricker and, even though it's Venue It has a touch of Mercury to it , too. It initially smells soft and smooth, but beneath there is a distinct more arousing and busy character. It shares the traits of Mercury in that it can smooth and blend different scents and create an ideal blend when paired with different scents. It is sometimes referred to as sweetcane and is found in recipes for kyphi. It is used in perfume oils that have an Egyptian tilt. It is an ingredient in Van Van Oil and is perfect for focusing your attention on the ritual of love or magic.

The aroma of the palmarosa blends will blend with the scents of rosewood, sandalwood patchouli, rose, petitgrain oakmoss, neroli lemongrass, mandarin jasmine, guaiacwood and geranium. Also, frankincense, citronella, clovebud and chamomile. Also, cedar, cananga and cassia. They also have black pepper and Amyris.

Lemon

Lemons were used for centuries by Romans, Egyptians, and Indians to treat infections. Lemons aren't only used to make lemonade anymore.

The lemon is associated with lunar cycles and the water. They are usually used in celebrations to honor lunar gods. It is extremely cleansing and cleansing. It can be used to cleanse your skin or as an ritual bath. It is possible to include the oil or leaf in water to cleanse your home. It is commonly used in love spells and it can be added to baked goods to show your love intentions.

It can also be used to treat ailments as well. Juice from a fresh lemon can be mixed with six ounces water to make a cleanser that is recommended to consume twice each daily. It can also aid in digestion by aiding in cleansing your digestive system. It stimulates the liver and removes toxins from it particularly the uric acid. It also assists in supporting the immune system, and helps with women who have excessive menstrual flow and rheumatism.

It is often added to hot water along with honey to ease sore throats, congestion colds and fevers.

Lavender

Lavender is a great herb to soothe the nerves, reduce stress, function as an antidepressant and anxiolytic and can help with sleep disorders. Lavender sachets that are kept close to your bed can help you sleep better and have delightful and sweet sleep. It is possible to achieve the same effect by burning oil.

Lavender is believed to be associated to air and Mercury It is also associated with Mercury and air, and also with the gods Hecate as well as Mercury Hermes. It is well-known for its attractiveness and sexual arousal force. Prostitutes would wear it to attract potential clients and make themselves appear more attractive.

It is often used in spells to help with dreams, to summon Hecate or Hermes communicate with the entities Send messages, eject dead people, fight the eye of evil, long-term health and healing beauty, love attraction, luck and cleansing.

It is an extremely distinctive and varied oil and herb within the Wiccan world. It is a useful ingredient in virtually every spell out there. This is an important herb and oil that you must keep in your bag.

Juniper

Juniper is masculine, and is connected to Jupiter along with fire. It is believed to be an herb of protection that helps in preventing theft. A sprig of rosemary on your body is believed to safeguard yourself from attacks by animals as well as accidents. If you put one on your front door, it can safeguard your home from the bad forces and other people.

It is frequently utilized to draw good energy as well as to eliminate curses and hexes. It can also help with psychic powers, as well as even used for exorcisms. When you combine it with amulets or a love mix it will help men increase their potential. You can make use of dried juniper berries in the making of amulets or charms.

Incense made of Juniper is beneficial in performing rituals that are aimed at manifesting or when you require lots of smoke.

Juniper is also used in smudging rituals to cleanse and bless homes and structures such as temples.

Clove

The clove spice is derived from an evergreen plant from the Molucca Islands in Indonesia. The dried flowers of the tree. It's been component of the herbalist's kit for quite a long period of. It functions as an antibacterial and anesthetic. It can be rubbed on gums in order to help relieve teeth and relieve pain.

Clove buds that are brewed into tea can aid with digestion , flatulence and ease nausea and diarrhea.

Cloves are linked to the fire element as well as Jupiter and are considered masculine. It is used to enhance prosperity as well as good luck, and friendship and gossip spells. Burning cloves can stop people from spreading negative reports about you.

Cinnamon

Cinnamon is well-integrated with kinds of plants and elements It can therefore be employed in spells which calls on air, fire, Uranus, Mars, Sun or Mercury. This was the very first crop to be used throughout the Eastern areas. It was burned to cleanse the temple.

In the realm of magic, it is most often used for psychic growth protection as well as happiness and peace. It is also used to promote passion money, love luck, energy, consecration, divination, and the ability to see. In China it's an important cleanser. It should not be applied in direct contact with the skin since it could cause irritation. Cinnamon is often used in spells to protect because it symbolizes active energy source and is linked to the sun.

Similar to the reasons for which it is, it can also be used to boost prosperity too. If you mix cinnamon with other oil for prosperity like ginger, orange and cloves, it can create an enchanting potpourri that can help you boost your finances.

Since it is both fiery and hot, it is an ideal ingredient to make use of in romance and sex. You can grind the cinnamon stick, mix it in equal parts myrrh and sandalwood. then burn it to create an incense for boosting your relationship.

Cinnamon powder is widely used to create prosperity to businesses. Shop owners can put sugar and cinnamon on their front steps to bring the business. The cinnamon powder can assist you in winning games.

Cedar Wood

Cedarwood oil is often associated with the sun and male gods. It is an excellent oil to put in an aroma that honors sun gods. A lot of people make use of cedarwood as a charm to earn money. In China they consider these trees as lovers due to of the way that their branches grow when two trees are close to each other.

Inanna the goddess of love from Assyrian mythology was believed to have eaten some of the trees in order to acquire sexuality and knowledge of love. In Britain this tree can be regarded as a signpost to death when it sheds its branches. Also, it is believed to inspire the power of angels, particularly when a person requires help. This is the reason it's used in a range of spells.

In Roman period, Celts would embalm their opponents' heads using cedar wood oil in order they could preserve and preserve their heads.

Cedarwood oil blends well with ylang-ylang and vetiver. tonka bean, sandalwood rosewood, rosemary and chamomile, pine orris, palmarosa, petitgrain myrrh, marjoram lavender and labdanum. It also works well with the juniper berry, frankincense clary sage and fir cardamom, cassia, bay leaf, bergamot amyris, anise and Ambrette.

Bergamot

Bergamot is an essential oil which is masculine and linked to the air element along with the star Mercury. It is among the primary ingredients in the scent of eau de cologne. It's also a mild oil, which makes it suitable for use on the skin.

It's great for treating insects repellent, cystitis stress, as well as digestive problems. It can also be used as a deodorant, tonic and antidepressant. It also acts as a stimulant, diuretic and analgesic.

Magically, it could be used to help ease anxiety, promote restful sleep and happiness. It can also bring peace. It is often used for relaxation and purifying spells. For relaxation or to eliminate the hex, add you can add some to add to a warm bath.

It is possible to gain wealth by putting an empty leaf in your wallet or purse. Prior to an interview make sure to rub your hands over the leaves to attract luck. Keep a sachet of leaves around you every time you gamble to attract luck. It can also help you attract the success you desire.

Incense from Bergamot is used to increase motivation, assertiveness and courage. It also helps to build strength as well as balance, confidence focus, alertness safety, pleasure, lift spirits, wealth and money.

How do you mix oils

After you've gathered the vast amount of information available regarding oils, you're likely to be wondering what you can do to blend your own oils. There are oils that are known as synergy mixes that have already mixed a number of essential oils to suit your needs. Although they are practical, they might not offer what you're looking for.

Mixing your own style will allow you to save money. It will also help you gain confidence in your abilities and practice. Before we get started mixing your oils, you must go over some essential facts first.

Before beginning any project, consider this trio of questions

1. What are the reasons you're looking to blend your oils?

2. What are their purpose?

3. What do you think you will do making use of your blend?

It is important to determine these questions before purchasing the first essential oil. You'll need a variety of oils to make a blend which will be used to help love, and then the blend is intended to boost your prosperity. This is similar to shopping for food items. You wouldn't visit the grocery store without knowing what you're going to require, so you shouldn't go shopping for oils until you are aware of what you'll use the products.

If you're about to purchase oil, ensure that you buy high-quality oils. If you're not sure what this means, then you should go back a few chapters. This is vital due to the fact that low-quality essential oils resulting in bad blends that can result in bad effects.

Apart from knowing how to locate high-quality oils, it is also important to be aware of the kinds of oils you'll require in relation to the characteristics they offer. It's a simple process. You've probably already heard little about the 13 oils we discussed earlier. To find every other one, you need to do is search them.

Let's suppose you want to make a blend of oils that can be used to heal. The essential oils you'd require are:

*Tea tree (Melaleuca alternifolia)
* Sandalwood (Santalum album)
* Rosemary (Rosmarinus officinalis)
*Peppermint (Menta Piperita)
* Oregano (Origanum vulgare)
* Lemon (Citrus limon)
* Lavender (Lavandula Angustifolia)
* Frankincense (Boswellia Carteri)
* Eucalyptus (Eucalyptus Globulus)
* Clove (Eugenia caryophyllata)

These are all distinctive oils with healing properties. There are a variety of other oils available which can be utilized as a healing synergy blend too.

The next step is to determine which oils you're planning to blend. It may be difficult but it's actually not that difficult. All you need to do is select oils that are healing and have a note that are component of that class. This will ensure that once they're blended, they leave a pleasant scent. This is particularly important in the event that you are planning to use the aromatherapy blends or for healing, however, if you're making them into spells, it's not so crucial. Still, I'd prefer to smell good while performing spells.

To assist you to help you, let's examine the various categories and how they mix with each other.

* Citrus (lime lemon, lime,) Blends well with spicy, oriental and woodsy scents, as well as minty and floral
* Oriental (Patchouli, Ginger) It blends well with spicy, citrus woodsy, and floral
* Hot (Cinnamon clove, cinnamon) Blends well with oriental, citrus woodsy, floral, and oriental
* The medicinal (tea tree, cajuput and Eucalyptus) Blends well with woodsy
* Minty (spearmint peppermint) Blends well with herbaceous, citrus, woodsy and earthy
* Herbaceous (basil marjoram, rosemary, basil) Blends well with mint, and woodsy

* Earthy (patchouli as well as vetiver, oakmoss, and patchouli) It blends well with mint and woodsy

* Woodsy (cedar pine) Blends well with oriental, citrus and spicy. It is also herbal, minty and earthy

* Floral (jasmine and neroli) Blends well with spicy, citrus, and woodsy

The aromas that essential oils have are determined by how quickly they disappear. If you apply a blend to your skin , it'll be a specific scent, and then , a few hours later, it'll have a different scent. This is due to the fact that some oils have been evaporated. Notes like these are known in the form of top, middle or base notes. There's quite a long list of different notes in oil, but I'll offer an example using the sample of the list I mentioned earlier.

The top notes: Peppermint and Lemon. Lavender and Eucalyptus

Middle Notes Tea Tree, Rosemary, Oregano, and Clove

The Base Notes are: Sandalwood and Frankincense

When you are first beginning to blend it is recommended to start with three oils: the top, middle and base. The more you're comfortable and the more oils you'll be able to start mixing.

Picking a Base

Once you begin mixing it, you'll find that several recipes require the base oil as well as a carrier oil. Carrier oils usually come from nuts or seeds of diverse plant species. They aid in diluting essential oils that are extremely strong and may be dangerous to handle. This also prevents your oils from degrading rapidly.

The purchase of a high-quality carrier oil is as essential as purchasing a top essential oil of high-quality. Pure, unrefined cold-pressed oils without additives are the top.

Coconut oil - This is a great carrier oil if you are planning to apply any of the blends you have chosen for your skin. It's safe for all skin types and accessible to locate. Remember that it will remain in a solid state when it's kept the temperature of 76 or less. It won't work in the event that you require your blend in liquid form, therefore you'll have to choose another option and mix it in with a different carrier oil.

Avocado oil is another fantastic option. If you're in a place where avocado oil is available the avocado oil may be a bit harder to locate. It's a more thick oil to ensure that it doesn't be able to run as quickly.

Almond oil is safe for almost all skin types, except if you have an allergy to almonds. It is also dependent on the location you reside in as to the ease to locate. The oil is liquid, which makes it the ideal choice for oil to apply an anoint.

Argan oil – this is relatively easy to locate. It's not the ideal oil for mixing however it is a good choice.

Olive oil is probably the most convenient and the most affordable option. It's safe for virtually every skin type. It's the most sought-after choice of carrier oils.

Supplies

There aren't a lot of items to begin mixing. In fact, you likely already have everything you need within your house right now.

Essential collection of oils

Pen and paper are great to record your experiment

* Gloves

• Cotton balls that you can smell your creation If you're interested in scenting good

Glass dropper or reducer cap

* Blending bottle or small glass container that has secured lid

Proportions

If you're not making any recipe and are simply experimenting, it's best to begin with a minimum of ten drops your oils to ensure that you don't waste the oil while testing. Once you begin the experiment, you'll have any carrier oils.

The most common method of dividing your oils is 30, 50, 20. This implies 30 percent of your blend will make up your high note 50 percent of your blend is your middle note and 20% of your blend will serve as your baseline note. Be aware that this doesn't include the carrier oil. This is due to how the oils evaporate.

A good example of a healing blend could be:
3 drops peppermint
5 drops of rosemary
2 drops frankincense

Blending

Once you've figured out the one of the most crucial aspects of blending Let's take a look at the procedure you should follow when you are experimenting with your blends. Be sure to not use the carrier oil.

At first, you'll need to do the same thing over and over until you are able to master it. of it.

Start small and use just three oils: starting with a top, middle and base. Use drops 3 2, 5, and 3 while you experiment. Note your first impressions of the smell.

Once you've mixed the three oils that you would like to experiment with, leave them to rest within the glass vials for one couple of days. This gives them time to mix and get a harmonious blend to let you know the quality of their mix.

Once it's had the chance to rest, you can try the sniff test. Put a small amount of the fragrance on a test strip or a cotton ball , and let the scent inhale. Jot in a few notes. Things like whether you enjoyed the smell, what emotions it brought up, and other others like that. Check if the scent has changed since the first time you mixing it.

If you are satisfied with what you have, blend it up with a pleasant-smelling carrier oil. Four drops of the ten drops of mixture gives you 20 percent reduction. Take note of how this changes the smell. If you like the scent you've created, place an label on it, and keep it in a cool, dark place to be used in the future. You may also expand the recipe to create large quantities.

Chapter 9: Using Stones And Crystals In Wicca

"Come Fairies, lift me from this dull world I'd love to ride along with you on the breeze and dance on the mountains as if I were a flame!"

William Butler Yeats

The entire world of healing stones, crystals, and semi-precious stones is a source of energy that is powerful, located deep within Earth's core. The word"gemstone" is associated with energy and strength along with wealth and lust as well as nature and magick. The people who use them would do so for a myriad of reasons such as healing and meditation to recharge oneself with positive energy, and developing insight and dedication. These stones can also be employed as talismans and amulets because they have energies and vibration frequencies.

In magical rituals they are often used to aid in healing, as amulets, an energy source for healing and as a way to increase the power. In rituals, hold your favorite gemstone in your palm, place it in your eyes and pay attention to the energy it carries. Be aware of how it is flowing throughout your body.

Every stone serves a purpose when it comes to magical rituals:

Sapphire is a stone that typically is found in dark blue colors However, it can be available in green, yellow black and gray.

Blue Sapphire

Is connected to the Saturn. Saturn. It's a stone of that symbolizes aristocracy, wisdom, loyalty and strength. This stone is thought to be a source of loyalty, aristocracy and can increase the longevity of eyesight and longevity. It also helps treat skin issues, cancer and insomnia. It also helps you remain on the spiritual path and keep a high level of concentration on your own goals. The blue hue of Sapphire can also help you awaken and activate it's Throat as well as the Third Eye Chakra.

Ruby

It is associated with our most powerful star which is the Sun. It is a reddish color. is a stone of opulence and purity, as well as high energy as well as leadership and prosperity. Ruby enhances our vitality (chi also known as prana) It also protects us from unhappy times and assists in decision making and goal-setting. Ruby is also a great way to increase heart power, boosts the performance of the circulatory system, speeds up elimination, and helps protect the kidneys, embryo, and eyes. It is closely linked to the chakra that is the root and helps open this chakra.

Moonstone

Like the moon, it is a symbol of mystery, the moon also has the power to be awe-. As represented by the Moon It is a stone that promotes calmness spirituality, inner explorations, along with new start-ups. Moonstone enhances sensitivity, intuition and helps to treat obesity and water retention as well as hormonal imbalances. Moonstone also has beneficial effects for those who suffer from depression and anxiety. This stone awakens the energy of kundalini and can bring out the best in people. As a Goddess-like stone It connects the spirit and energy of Nature. It can be worn as a talisman in order to increase and strengthen the character of the wearer.

Tiger eye

The planet Mercury is the source of the stone. Mercury. The Tiger Eye is known for its power to manifest, luck as well as protection. It assists in the regenerating of energy within the body. it rejuvenates cells and helps reduce the convulsions, pains, and toxicity that is found in the body. It is also beneficial in the treatment with anemia and throat problems. Tiger eye is known for its spiritual properties and assists in connecting and communicating between your children, as well as protects you from evil spirits. Aids in the manifestation of abundance and wealth within the physical world and it has significant positive impacts upon chakras like the Root as well as the Solar Plexus chakras.

For the best outcomes, you can create your own crystal or stone that contains your own energy. In the course of the ritual, you should place the stone in your hands and imagine that it is charged with your energy as well as the energies of God and goddess. It is possible to write or think about it to give an intention specific to the stone. The reason for this can be financial protection, protection or health, or something else.

It is important to remember to keep your stones clean regularly. You can put them in the ground for up to 24 hours or let them outside in the night. Whichever option you pick make sure you are aware of your stones since they're part of you, they are your world, and contain your energy.

Once you've used them for a certain period such as a few years, think about giving them back with Mother Earth. Bring them back to the soil. Remember that you are able to start fresh , with a new attitude and a vision for your life and your future.

Chapter 10: Utilizing Oils In Witchcraft

A Combination of Earth's Element of Water

Oils are very easy and easy to incorporate into your magical rituals and everyday rituals. They are able to assist you in attracting the things you desire and require within your own life. Imagine what you would like or require in your life. Then at this point, place some drops of oil into the burner. The drops of oil do not ignite but they are instantly heated and disappear and release their scents into the air. In this process it is beneficial to use spells in chanting to boost the effect in the ceremony. Here's an example of an effective spell that you can employ or note down your own magick rituals that increase the power.

There is a Wicca tradition and religion is a bigger belief in the oil's power. To extract oil from your favourite plant or herb You need to wrap your herbs in cheesecloth before putting it in a jar filled with coconut oil, olive oil or almond oil, as well as any other oils you prefer. It should be left for 20 to 35 hours in sun. And make sure to shake the jar at least once every day. The herb extract you choose will be absorbed into base oils giving it the scent of nature.

Chapter 11: Utilizing Plants And Herbs In Witchcraft

,,Magic(k) cannot be a method of practice. It is an ever-growing, living web of energy, which is, with our permission it can surround us in every move."

Dorothy Morrison

Through time, Witches have gained substantial understanding of plants and herbs and their application in healing and magick. Today, Wiccans and Witches use their understanding of plants and herbs during rituals as well as in healing. Magick is the way they remain connected to Nature.

Plants and herbs have numerous applications, some of these are:

Bath salts

The two Witches and Wiccans create their own bath salts by grinding and mixing herbs, in conjunction together with Epsom salt or another salt you like.

They make use of this mix prior to doing rituals to cleanse their bodies and their energy.

Sachets

Witches make perfume by mixing herbs and putting them in bags, typically made of silk , so they can wear them or carry it as an amulet in their pockets or even under their pillow.

Incense

Incense is made by mixing herbs that are harvested, dried and then blended. Incense is utilized for burning in rituals.

Some herbs that have been specifically chosen for their uses

Herbs are used for specific reasons within the celebrations, rituals and customs of Wicca. There's plenty to discuss in this area, to get more information, I would suggest that you purchase Scott Cunningham's book about Herbs.

* Jasmine can be used to bring more physical and financial wealth in the life of your Love, happiness, and improved sleeping.

* Mustard is a spice used for the enhancement of mental and fertility.

* Parsley is great for purification as well as for protection. Rose is well-known for its role in the performance of love rituals. Violet is a good choice for protection from the spiritual realm for luck, protection, and healing.

The Dandelion flower is utilized to call spirits and connecting to Divination.

Frankincense is a great choice for removing negative energy. It can also be used to establish connections to your mind and astral realm.

* Ginseng is ideal for love, lust and for healing.

You may choose to plant your own plants and herbs or to purchase the plants from a herbalist. But, the most important thing to remember is be mindful of the possible allergies that you or your family members may suffer from with regard to the plants. Be mindful about the possibility that dried herbs can be hazardous to your health, when you're allergic to these herbs. The second important thing is to be aware of the herbs that are toxic. You shouldn't come into contact with them and be careful not to consume them through smoking or drinking. The most effective way to avoid them is to substitute the herbs with different ones.

Make use of your own oils with candles to get the best outcomes from your magical experience. Incense is burned while performing the ritual, and draw the circle in a clockwise direction to protect yourself. Inhale the incense's smoke to cleanse your home free of negativity. Also, make sure the windows are shut. While you travel from one area to another, think about the following phrases.

Negative energy, you can not be able to stay. Goddess free the negative energies from me and move them off.

Alongside cleansing your home from negative energy and chanting contemplate putting herbs in a protective place all over the home.

Chapter 12: The Right Timing For Performing Rituals

The goal of our lives is living in harmony with the natural world."

Zeno

When we imagine magick, the image that is in front of us typically involves the nighttime rituals that we perform. However, as I mentioned earlier, Wiccan God is represented by the Sun and the Sunlight. It is your choice to conduct a ritual at any time you believe that the time is right for you, regardless of whether it's in the evening or during the daytime.

Magick ritual at dawn

Dawn itself is a magical time of the day it is a time of the day when the day slowly wakes up while the night sky appears half-bright halfway dark. It's the ideal moment to think about new ideas, new beginnings and spiritual renewal. The past was when witches would gather plants before dawn to create love potion.

Magick rituals at Noon

The energy of God can be at its highest and strongest during this time. There's a lot of energy that you can use to perform your rituals of magick. Make use of this energy to increase your strength and tackle any the issues you believe you require to get over. Let the universe be a part of your success.

Magick ritual that takes place at Dusk

The day's light is coming to an end, and the dark night is slowly creeping up. This is the time that the gates of the magical world are open and performing rituals of magick during this time period will give you access to all realms. The frequency of communication with divine energies is extremely powerful.

Magick nighttime ritual

The Goddess' energy is strong in the night. You can now look back on the day's events, and focus on only the positive aspects of your life. This energy can be used to cast spells and bring more positive events into your life.

Midnight magick ritual

Also called Witch Hour represents the perfect time to connect to Goddess and soak up the energies associated with the Moon. It's the perfect opportunity to connect with your intuition and to connect with your personal world. Make a ritual and use a spell to remove all negativity and gain the healing power from the Universe. Lighting a candle in the memory to God of the Horned God or Goddess, and remain silent. Then you will be able to hear the wisdom of. Request her advice and guidance and ask her to be a part of with you and when the moon is shining brightly, ask the Goddess to illuminate your path. This is the time to are able to feel and accept her powerful presence. If you ask, you will receive. We have endless possibilities. The problem is that most people don't realize their opportunity.

Chapter 13: Designing Your Own Magickal Journal - Your Most Trusted Accountability Partner

Through the ages Witches have recorded the results of every spell they have performed, every ritual they've conducted as well as the plant-based remedies and cures crystals, oils, crystals, as well as all their information about their knowledge of the Universe, Nature and their ways of living. To safeguard their traditions, their way of life and their legacy, they utilized their Runic alphabet to record their experiences in their books. The current edition is the "Book of Shadows,"" "Book of Magick" or "Grimoire," it should be read every day by each Wicca user or Witch.

It is possible to create the process of creating your personal Book of Shadows just by recording your thoughts about your emotions, beliefs, feelings and ideas for rituals on a regular basis. Write down the guidelines you wish to follow, but they should not be in the habit of harming other human beings. If you're a member of an organization called a coven and you follow a rulebook, you are able to write about these standards.

Write about your experience with the God and Goddess and how you think about them, how do you view and describe them, and what they mean to you. Write about the emotions you experienced when you first made the decision to devote all your efforts to Wicca. You can make Your Book of Shadows more practical by recording the different phases of the Moon, Sabbats, and Esbats rituals. You could write about your favourite crystals and how you feel connected to them, as well as the essential oils, herbs and candles. Think about writing about more personal issues as well as your rituals and changes you experience after a few months of doing these rituals. Write about your blessings and spells. Make a note of your visions and symbols since this is the method by which God and Goddess communicate with you.

It's your own individual Book of Shadows so feel free to express yourself fully. Be careful to keep it private and only share your secrets with people who are like you or not one else if that is more your style. You individual Book of Shadows will be the most precious thing you own and an instrument for self-awareness as well as development as a an integral part of Wicca tradition.

Chapter 14: Tools For Wicca Practitioner

If you believe that Wicca is the right choice for you and you are looking to learn more about the art, you don't have to spend a fortune to purchase all of the items available in this article or via the Internet.

You are free to begin with the simplest items and things you can get at a lower cost.

Begin with candles since they are relatively inexpensive and come in a variety of sizes, colors, and shapes. Candle holders can be purchased and found at a reasonable cost. You may try your hand at making one yourself and try creating one of your own. Anything you create will be legal even if you don't adhere to all the "rules."

Gemstones and crystals are utilized in magick. It is not necessary to buy a huge amount of crystals in one go. Begin with just a few to discover how you can connect with them. They are all over the world so your selection will increase with time.

Divination tools: tarot cards, oracles, runes, etc. They are utilized to make choices, enhancing your psychic abilities , and finding important answers. The most effective Tarot deck that I have used is the Thoth Deck. For more details, click here.

Feathers are necessary, but you don't have to buy them as they is available in the form of a cone or powder, and symbolizes the element easily locate them on your own. The feather symbolizes the element Air. It is a type of Air. It is also employed as Air Magick.

holy water can be used to cleanse your magical objects.

The pentacle may be utilized as a pendant but you may also place it on your altar to ensure protection. Noting that The four Pentagram's points are the components: Earth, Air, Water, and Fire. The fifth symbolizes the Spirit.

Salt is a symbol from the Earth and is used to create holy water to aid in magick.

* Music is used as a part of rituals. It's an amazing instrument for raising your own vibrational energy and is utilized in

meditation to calm your mind and calming the spirit. You can listen to music while you perform an ritual or your favourite sacred dance.

A wand is a tool utilized to direct energy in rituals, and is made using a variety of materials. The athame (ritual dagger) is a crucial tool that can help focus your power to where it's required.

Chapter 15: Magical Circle And Sacred Altar

If you're new to Witchcraft and Wicca and are looking to carry out a ritual of magick The first thing you should master is to learn how to cast an esoteric circle. This is, thankfully, the easiest to learn and is also the most crucial. It's quite normal and is also among the top crucial aspects of rituals. Casting circles will shield you safe from harmful and destructive energy.

Find a suitable location to have your wedding, outdoors or indoors and select an appropriate time to know that you won't be at risk of being disturbed.

Clean the area thoroughly and make use of your wand or Broom to remove negativity from your area. Incense can also be used to accomplish this. Crystals can be used to create a circle or sprinkle salt. You could draw a circle using your athame. Or, you could light candles and make a ring using candles. If you choose to conduct your ritual outdoors then you could utilize branches or rocks to achieve the same effect. When casting your circle you should move slowly and visualize a huge circle of positive energy surrounding you. You can also imagine the circle you cast as magical web that expands around you.

Keep in mind that the circle, once formed, is not damaged until after the ceremony has been carried out. This is why you must bring everything you'll need to carry inside the circle. If you have to exit the circle you can use your athame create a magical door. Never cut the whole circle. The Altar is an altar where you honor Your God or Goddess. Cast spells and meditate, make offerings, etc.

After everything is set when everything is ready, place your altar in the direction of North.

It is recommended that the God things should sit on the right side , and the Goddess items should be placed on the side to left.

These are the products that you'll use the most frequently during your rituals:

Two candles represent God and Goddess

*One God statue as well as one Goddess statue

* A plate to serve offerings

Chapter 16: Ritual To Destroy The Negativity That Is A Part Of Your Life

"Remember Heaven as Father to you, Earth as your Mother and all that is alive as your Sister and Brother."

Native Wisdom

Everyone has been through the highs and lows of life. Most of us have experienced negative moods do not last for long, but if are caught in a cycle with negative thought patterns, it's time to take a step back and take control of your life. If you have reason to think the person who casts a curse over you, don't rush to cast it back. Be mindful of that the Law of Three. If you are in this situation If someone has put a spell on you, or you're going through difficult times within your own life it's time to do the magick process to melt off all negative energy. The Elements are there to assist anyone who would be willing to ask.

To use an element that is fire you'll require an ember. It is recommended to make use of a black candle.

Make sure you clean your mind and try to relax as you possibly can, or otherwise anger, thoughts of negativity and frustrations could easily spill over into your physical energy and hinder your work.

Lighting the candle and imagining it that it represents your negative situation that you are trying to resolve. As it burns, think:

"Spirits of the flame take my advice and follow my instructions
Burn the candle, and burn my bad luck
Support me in my life's journey."

If you'd like to approach Air to help you get rid of negative energy that is affecting your life, you can simply grab one piece of paper and record your situation. Record everything that is not helping you achieve your goals and living more joyful life. When you're done burning the paper, then throw the ashes in the wind. Then, ask the Air element Air to help you:

"Power from wind and air
Burn these ashes far from me.
can cause harm to anyone, however it may."

It is possible to harness waters power in order to rid yourself of negative energy that has accumulated in your life. So this ritual is fantastic when you live close to the shores of a river or lake.

On the stone or paper write the things you would like to rid yourself of take a walk near the water and invoke water as the element Water as you toss the paper into.

"Spirits of water aid me get rid of negative thoughts

And bad luck and misfortune in my personal life when your water runs away

might be that things that don't serve me in the long run are further away

Water spirits hear my words and take away my words.

my bad luck I will not harm anyone and do what I want to."

It is also possible to perform the bath ritual, and while doing so, invoke waters elements to cleanse the bad luck It's not necessary. Imagine how all negative energies disappear from your body. It is the most receptive element, it can be charged by expressing your desire and energy.

When you make a decision to rid yourself of negative energy within your life, don't forget to acknowledge the forces for their assistance on your way.

Chapter 17: The Journey Of The Witch: Walking A Path Of Wicca

"The true pagan doesn't have any requirement of religion as no matter what religion provides the pagan already has it." Osho

You've come a long way in the past, and are considering becoming an Witch and following through the paths of Wicca. It might appear to be a simple and enjoyable task But don't rush to any conclusions yet. There are obligations and personal responsibilities that you should keep in mind. It's an interesting book but you should commit yourself to reading other books too to increase your understanding of Wicca. It will teach you in greater details about rituals, deities as well as holidays and covens as well as being a solo practitioner, the practice of magick, history of magical spells and the elemental and the natural world. As you learn more and experience, you can decide your own self if Wicca is a path that you would like to pursue within your daily life.

As witches, you'll be entrusted with many duties, such as taking care of Nature as well as living creatures in your daily life. Make yourself capable of joining the coven. Be respectful of the beliefs of other people and don't force your views on others. You may choose to join Wicca at some point however, you shouldn't attempt to force your family members and friends to join at their own will.

The path to Wicca as well as living the lifestyle of being a Witch requires confidence to bring about changes to your daily life. If you've taken the plunge and want to live your the life of an Witch One of the most crucial actions you must take is face your inner self and confront your dark side.

A life as a Witch is mostly about self-awareness, ability to confront what you are, and to reflect about your past. It's essential in the process of making changes and becoming more of a person. One of the essential aspects that make a good witch is to be silent. It is essential to avoid getting too emotional. it will happen naturally as you progress, grow and become better at your craft. It is essential to be quiet about the work you do. You should recognize the damaging power of the Ego If it is not managed in check. If it's not hidden then it's not really magick.

Make use of your powers wisely and do magick that can assist in making this world more peaceful. We're all aware of the destruction that humanity has created for itself, and as an Witch you have to be a catalyst for positive change, however the change you make may be small. Join in the making of light on earth.

The last thing to do is believe in your capabilities. Believe in yourself, the path you've chosen and your magical work. Bring your heartfelt desire for the world to be better with your own energies and elements. This is the only way to build a better world.

Chapter 18: Wiccan Candle Magick

"Witchcraft ... can be described as an enlightening path. It's a way to get spiritual nourishment and to connect with the vital power of the universe and to better understand your life."

Christopher Penczak

The time has come for what's fun. Candle Spells are among the most simple types of casting spells. It's a type of magic that doesn't require the caster to engage in any elaborate ritual. This type of magic doesn't require use of costly ritual instruments or artifacts. Anyone can perform candle magick. If you're not convinced, consider it as a moment of contemplation. Rememberthose moments on your birthday when you made wishes and then blew out the candles from your cake? The same principle applies. In this instance instead of waiting for an event to occur the ceremony is a declaration of your commitment to it. If you think about it in a more clear way The lighting of the candle on the cake ceremony has three basic concepts:

1. Determine what your goal will be.
2. Imagine what the end result will look
3. Completely commit to this outcome

What Candles Do You Need?

Many who perform candle magic probably tell you that, as with other life's crucial aspects, size doesn't really matter. The phrase "The biggerthe candle, the more powerful" isn't the case to this situation. In reality, the use of a candle that is too large could be a bit ineffective. This is due to the fact that certain candle spells require instructing the spellcaster to hold off until the flame burns its own out before carrying on to the next casting to invoke the spell. Thus, using an oblong or a votive candle is suggested.

There will be instances when a particular type of candle is needed for an occult spell, like the 7-day candle or a figure candle that represents a particular person. It's awe-inspiring to learn that among the best candles used for the ritual of chanting magic is the Menorah candle.

A key thing to remember while using candlelight is to to ensure that you have use a brand new candle to spellwork - virgin materials.

Never use any leftover candles left over from previous spellwork. The belief of the magical world is that when a candle is lit, it creates energy from all that surrounds it. It is best to light a new candle to ensure a magical result. If you intend to use spells to accomplish different goals it is an ideal idea to use candles with various shades. Each candle color represents different kinds of magic that candles can perform. Here are a few examples:

Pink = Love and Friendship

* Orange: Attraction and Encouragement

* Red Heart: Lust, Love, Courage Health

* Yellow: Persuasion, protection and protection

* Green: Abundance, Fertility, Green Great potential for financial gain

* Gold: Solar connections, good business opportunities, tremendous wealth

* Dark Blue: Resistance depression and anxiety.

* Purple is a symbol of ambition and power.
"Light Blue": understanding good health, and patience
* Black: Banishment, Negativity, restriction
* White Pure Truth: Truth, and tranquility
* Brown: Nature-related (Earth and animals) functionings
* Silver Lunar Connections, Reflection, and the intuition

Remember that in certain Pagan practices, white candles are thought to be universal. This means it is a alternative to any color.

Wiccan Spell #1:
Basic Money Spell
Pick an unopened, small new candle, and then dress in oil. Be sure the dressing oil you use is genuine. Charge the candle dressed using your personal intentions to cast the spell.
* Pick small pieces of paper and record your desire to enjoy lots of wealth, luck and prosperity. Concentrate on your goal as much as you can while writing in all the lines on the paper. Also, ensure that your

document is of the same hue that the candle you're using.

* Light the candle. As you light your candle, you're picturing that your wish will come to fruition.

After spending an amount of time contemplating different shapes, your ideals could be realized folded piece of paper, and then ignite it with the flame of the candle.

* Hold the paper in flames for as long as is possible, but be sure you aren't burning your fingers in the process. Put it in a fireproof bowl or caldron, and allow it to fully burn.

• Leave the candle burning in its own way until it has completely burned itself out. Here is another variant that uses a spell which can improve one's financial position. This spell doesn't just bring riches, but also wealth.

Wiccan Spell #2:
Spell for Prosperity and Wealth

* To make this happen you'll need two brand new candles in two distinct colors: gold and green.

* When the moon is at its waning phase on a Thursday night begin casting this spell. It is crucial to start this spell only at the waning of the moon on the night of a Thursday.

Use money oils to rub the candles, then begin charging them with your own personal energy.

* Draw"prosperity, "prosperity" onto one candle, and "money" onto the second candle.

• Light the candles and then hold them in a position where both your energy and the energy are interspersed.

* While you close your eyes Imagine the abundance of wealth and prosperity that is coming to you.

If you are imagining achieving your goal, repeat the following incantation verbatim: "Both of these candles will bring prosperity and wealth for me in a way that doesn't harm anyone else." Repeat it three times.

* After repeating the mantra three times, extinguish the flames.
* The candle is lit for a few minutes every night until the candle has burned completely.

Wiccan Spell #3:
Confidence Candle Spell
In order to make it happen, you'll need these items:
* Roses in pink and white petals

Pure or fresh water Pure is the best choice in this situation. However, if you're completely comfortable drinking rainwater then a bottle of spring water is sufficient. It is possible to make use of tap water in the event of a need, but it's not recommended.

Conclusion

Wicca in all forms is important to a large number of people. At the conclusion in this text, you might find yourself thinking it that Wicca is a way of life you'd like to try. It doesn't matter if you remain a single practitioner or join a circle, coven, or are an High Priest or Priestess in the practice in British Traditional Wicca, your journey is bound to be full of excitement and exploration. Spiritual growth and personal development and experience of the Mystery and spiritual connection with gods of the past, and connections to others who experience the world the same way you do the many benefits that come from Wiccan practice. With Wicca the possibilities for discovery are always just around the next corner. There is no ritual that is identical once, and every encounter with the gods is different. Individuality and creativity are praised, and inclusiveness is the hallmark. Witches are from every walk of life, all religions traditions, and from all economic backgrounds. Their experiences may differ however they all have a common belief that magic has the ability to create change throughout the world. Join Wicca and become a part of a group of love and spirituality.

Thank you for buying this book. Best of luck on your spiritual journey wherever it might take you!

www.ingramcontent.com/pod-product-compliance
Lightning Source LLC
Chambersburg PA
CBHW050411120526
44590CB00015B/1924